HOW TO USE A LAW LIBRARY

AUSTRALIA
The Law Book Company Ltd.
Sydney : Melbourne : Brisbane

CANADA AND U.S.A.
The Carswell Company Ltd.
Agincourt, Ontario

INDIA
N.M. Tripathi Private Ltd.
Bombay
and
Eastern Law House Private Ltd.
Calcutta

M.P.P. House
Bangalore

ISRAEL
Steimatzky's Agency Ltd.
Jerusalem : Tel Aviv : Haifa

MALAYSIA : SINGAPORE : BRUNEI
Malayan Law Journal (Pte.) Ltd.
Singapore

NEW ZEALAND
Sweet & Maxwell (N.Z.) Ltd.
Wellington

PAKISTAN
Pakistan Law House
Karachi

HOW TO USE
A LAW LIBRARY

by

JEAN DANE
Law Librarian, University College, Cardiff

and

PHILIP A. THOMAS
*Senior Lecturer in Law, University College,
Cardiff*

with specialist contributions on

Community Law

by
A.C. PAGE
*Lecturer in Law,
University College, Cardiff*

Public International
Law

by
A.V. LOWE
*Lecturer in Law,
University of Wales Institute
of Science and Technology,
Cardiff*

LONDON
SWEET & MAXWELL
1979

First Edition 1979
Second Impression 1980

Published by
Sweet & Maxwell Limited of
11 New Fetter Lane, London.
Computerset by Apex Computersetting,
London. Printed in Great Britain by
Page Bros. (Norwich) Limited.

ISBN Hardback 0 421 25250 2
Paperback 0 421 25260 X

INTRODUCTION

As a new student of law you will soon discover that all lecture and tutorial contact with the teaching staff results in you spending time in the law library. You may be preparing for a tutorial, reading references given during a lecture, or researching for an essay. One of the features of tertiary education is that far less time is occupied by group involvement with staff than was normal in secondary education. The emphasis is now upon personal commitment and effort. Academic staff will not spend their time chasing you for essays, attendance and diligent performance. The responsibility for this rests primarily with you. From this you will see that the task of discovering how the library is arranged, and how to use the materials in it, rests with you.

The study of law is essentially a library-based subject and you will spend a great deal of your time as a student in the law library. You will find that acquiring an effective working knowledge of the library will pay dividends, not only during your formal educational period but also in practice. Students who do not learn how to use the law collection and associated materials will be faced with difficulties in exercises, projects and essay preparation and, as a result, will find time spent in the library frustrating and relatively unproductive.

The purpose of this guide is to provide you with basic information about how a law collection is organised, administered and, more importantly, how it should be used. It will remain a useful reference source throughout your study period. It is not intended that you should treat it as a textbook to be read in conjunction with a particular course, but as a reference aid to be consulted whenever you are faced with a problem. Consequently, you might use the book selectively, referring to those sections which are useful at a particular point in your studies, or which are recommended by a lecturer. We consider this to be essentially a practical book, which tells you how to use the library materials properly. Consequently, the best place to read it is in the library, where you can see and handle the materials to which we refer. Lawyers carry only a limited amount of legal knowledge in their heads and a good lawyer is one who knows where to look for the relevant law and is then able to apply it successfully. This guide is intended to help you identify the relevant law relating to England and Wales. In addition, chapters have been provided outlining the sources of European Community law and public international law. Should you require more detailed information, this can be found in:

E. M. Moys, *Manual of Law Librarianship*

J. E. Pemberton, *British Official Publications* (2nd ed.)

D. J. Way, *The Student's Guide to Law Libraries* (a guide for articled clerks, trainee legal executives and Bar students)

M. A. Banks, *Using a Law Library* (2nd ed.) (emphasis on Canadian materials but has very useful chapters on English and American materials)

E. Campbell and D. MacDougall, *Legal Research: Materials and Methods* (emphasis on Australian sources)

M. O. Price and H. Bitner, *Effective Legal Research* (American sources)

University of London Institute of Advanced Legal Studies, *Manual of Legal Citations,* Parts I and II.

C. R. Lutyens, *Community Law*

British Institute of International and Comparative Law, *Where to Find Your Community Law* (2nd ed.)

Your introductory library tour, valuable though it is, usually takes place during the first, hectic week of your new life as a student. We hope that you will supplement this introduction by attempting the exercises we have set. Space is left after the question for you to fill in your answer and you can check the accuracy of your work by referring to the answers at the back of the book (Appendix IV). These questions have a two-fold purpose: first, to acquaint you with the physical appearance and location of the materials and, secondly to help you to understand how the materials can be used to find specific information. You might decide to ask a friend for the answers but you will not learn for yourself by this technique. We consider that some of the most important reference sources you will be referred to may be difficult to use. Consequently, in order to encourage understanding, we have also summarised how to use them. Additionally, we have introduced a number of flow-charts (algorithms). These are sets of questions, in visual, diagrammatic form which are structured in such a way as to provide you with a solution to your problem. Both the summaries and flow-charts are intended to be used in conjunction with the main text. Remember that the library staff are there to help you. If, after proper use of this book, you are still unable to find what you want do not hesitate to ask for assistance or information.

It is possible that not all the questions we have set can be answered, as the necessary materials may not be available in some libraries (although the questions are based on the basic library holdings recommended by the Society of Public Teachers of Law). The answers are, to the best of our knowledge, correct as of May 1978. Should you find mistakes or deficiencies, please notify us. We have had the benefit of advice from our colleagues, Dr. D. R. Miers (who also helped prepare the algorithms), Professor L. A. Sheridan, Ms Penny Smith, Mrs. K. Thompson, and Mr. A. Dashwood, who read the chapter on Community Law. We thank them for their suggestions and corrections.

December 1978   *Jean Dane*
                                                Philip A. Thomas

TABLE OF CONTENTS

CONTENTS

Contents

Contents

4. PERIODICALS

5. GOVERNMENT PUBLICATIONS

Contents

6. HOW TO FIND INFORMATION ON A SUBJECT

xiv

Contents

7. COMMUNITY LAW

8. PUBLIC INTERNATIONAL LAW

Contents

Contents

Chapter 1

USING A LIBRARY

1-1.   INTRODUCTION

When you first visit a large general library it can appear very confusing. However, most libraries are arranged on the same basic principles and once these have been mastered you should not experience too much difficulty in finding your way around, even in the largest library. A university, polytechnic or college library will contain two main types of material: books and periodicals (often called magazines or journals).

1-2.   BOOKS

1-3.   *Arrangement of Books on the Shelves*

Books are usually grouped on the shelves according to their subject. The subject dealt with in each book is indicated by numbers, or letters and numbers, which are usually written on the spine (or back) of the book. These symbols indicate the exact subject matter of each volume. They are known as the **classification number**. The purpose of the classification number is to bring together, in one area of the library, all books dealing with the same subject. The classification number serves two purposes. It indicates the subject of the book and tells you where the book is to be found on the shelves.

In some institutions, books on different subjects may be housed in separate buildings on the campus. For instance, you may find that the law books have been placed in a separate law library. If this has not been done, the law books will be collected (by means of the classification scheme) in one area of the general library.

There may be a number of separate sequences in the library. Some books, such as dictionaries and encyclopedias, are designed by their nature to be used as reference books, rather than as books to be read from cover to cover; these may be shelved in a reference area. Very large books (folios) and very thin books (pamphlets) may

1

be kept in a separate sequence. Thus, the size of the book may be important in helping you to find it on the shelves. There will normally be some indication on the catalogue entry (para. 1-4) if the book is shelved separately. Parliamentary papers and other official (government) publications are often located in an area of the library set aside for this purpose. Most important, from your point of view, there may be a separate reserve, short-term loan or undergraduate collection of basic textbooks which are in demand. These are normally available only for short periods of loan. Such a collection may include photocopies of articles from journals and extracts from books on your reading lists. The library may have some material (such as *The Times* newspaper) available only in the form of microfiche or microfilm, and there may be a collection of audio-visual material (cassettes, records, slides, etc.), press cuttings and other materials which do not form part of the normal book collection. Copies of examination papers set in previous years will often be available in the library.

1-4.   *Using the Library Catalogues to Find a Book*

To find out what books are available in the library you need to consult the catalogues, which are generally in a prominent position. The catalogue may consist of a number of drawers containing cards, there being a card for every book in the library. In some libraries the catalogue may be in the form of a looseleaf book, or sheets of computer print-out, or even a reel of microfilm, which you read with the aid of a special machine.

Whatever the physical format of the catalogue, there are usually two main sequences: an **author (or name) catalogue** and a **subject catalogue**. The author catalogue contains records, arranged alphabetically by the author's name, for all books in the library. The subject catalogue contains the same records but rearranged in subject order (so that entries for books on the same subject are together).

If you know the author's name, look up the surname in the author (or name) catalogue. The entries are arranged in alphabetical order by the author's surname. If there are several authors with the same surname, *e.g.* Smith, the entries are then filed by the authors' forenames or initials, *e.g.*

SMITH, A.B.
SMITH, Alan Norman
SMITH, Barbara

We have said that the arrangement of the entries is alphabetical. Unfortunately, this is not as simple as it seems. There are two ways of arranging entries in alphabetical order. One system is to arrange them "letter by letter," that is, as if they all form part of one long word, ignoring any spaces between words. The other arrangement is "word by word." You should find out which arrangement is used in your library, otherwise you can miss entries. This is shown by the change in the order of the following examples, using the two different filing methods. Publishers compiling indexes to books, and lists of the names of cases, may use either method.

Letter by Letter	*Word by Word*
Law Commission	Law Commission
Lawler, J.	Law Society
Lawrence, R. J.	Lawler, J.
Law Society	Lawrence, R. J.
Lawson, F. H.	Lawson, F. H.

When you have located the author's name, you will find an entry for every book by that author which is available in the library. The entries are arranged alphabetically by the titles of the books (ignoring words such as "The" or "A" at the beginning of the title). If a book has run into several editions, they will be arranged in order, with the latest edition at the back or at the front of the sequence (libraries vary in their practice on this point).

Suppose that you are looking for a book which continues to be known by the name of the original author, even though he is dead or no longer writing textbooks (and this is common practice in a law library). Let us take as an example, *Winfield and Jolowicz on Tort*. This is in its tenth edition. Winfield has not been involved with the work for many years, but it is still referred to by his name. You would, therefore, find an entry in the author catalogue under Winfield, but, in addition, there would also be an entry under Rogers, W. V. H., who is the author of the present edition.

Many well-known textbooks have been written jointly by two authors: Megarry and Wade (*The Law of Real Property*), Cross and

Jones (*Introduction to Criminal Law*) Smith and Hogan (*Criminal Law*), Cheshire and Fifoot (*The Law of Contract*) – these are standard works with whose names you will soon become familiar. If you are looking for the book by Cheshire and Fifoot, you can look in the author catalogue under either Cheshire or Fifoot, and you will find an entry in the catalogue under both names.

Sometimes a book does not appear to have an individual author. It has been published by an organisation or society and the organisation is, in effect, the author. In this case you will find an entry in the catalogue under the name of the body, *e.g.* Law Commission, Law Society, Legal Action Group, United Nations.

1-5.　　　　　　　*Finding a Book on the Shelves*

The **classification number** (para. 1-3) will appear prominently near the top of the catalogue entry. This number will enable you to trace the book on the shelves. If the library is a large one there should be, near the catalogue, a guide showing you where books with that classification number are to be found.

If you have any difficulty in understanding how the books are arranged on the shelves, or in using the catalogue, ask a member of the library staff for help.

If the book is not on the shelves it may be (a) in use by another reader in the library; (b) out on loan to another reader; (c) in a separate sequence of books which are larger or smaller than average, or which are in heavy demand (para. 1-3); (d) misshelved or missing; (e) removed by the library staff for some reason, *e.g.* rebinding. Ask the library staff at the issue desk (where you borrow books) if the book is on loan or if it is likely to have been removed from the shelves for any reason. If it is on loan, it may be possible for it to be recalled for you. If the book has been missing from the shelves for several days the library staff may institute a search for it or they may be able to suggest some other source from which you could obtain it.

1-6.　　　　　　　*Borrowing Books*

Assuming that you have located the book you require, how do you borrow it? It is not normally possible to borrow periodicals and law reports and some books may be available for loan for limited periods only, *e.g.* overnight or at weekends. This is because the law library is essentially a reference library and the material is in heavy demand. The library staff will explain how many books you may borrow, and how long you can keep them on loan. It is usually necessary for you to join the library, *i.e.* to provide details of your course, address, etc., before you borrow books. You may be issued with a library ticket which you must produce every time you borrow a book. The date of return will be stamped inside the book. Return it as soon as you have finished with it, or if the library asks for it. It is anti-social to retain books wanted by other readers and, as a result, you may be charged a fine if the book is returned late.

PROBLEMS

J. C. Smith is one of two authors of a book on criminal law. Look up his name in the catalogue and answer the following questions:

(a) Who is the other author of the book?

(b) Look up the entry under the other author's name in the catalogue and notice how it differs from the entry under Smith's name.

(c) What is the latest edition of the book which is available in your library?

(d) Who is the publisher of the book?

(e) In what year was it written?

(f) What is the classification number of the book?

(g) In what part of the library are books with this number to be found?

1-7.   LAW REPORTS AND PERIODICALS

In the course of your studies you will need to look at the reports of cases which have been heard in courts both in this country and

abroad. These reports are published in a number of publications
called **law reports**. Amongst the best known series of law reports
are the *All England Law Reports*, the *Weekly Law Reports* and the
Law Reports. We shall examine these series in more detail in
Chapter 2. The law reports are shelved in the law library and they
will often be grouped together by country, so that all the English
law reports are together. You may find that the international law
reports are shelved separately.

You will also find that you are referred to articles (essays) in
periodicals. Your reading list should give you the author and title
of the article, the year, the volume number, the title of the journal
in which the article appeared, and the first page number on which
the article is printed, *e.g.* Lloyd, "Do we need a Bill of Rights?"
(1976) 39 M.L.R. 121.

The form in which this information is written varies but it is
important that you should learn to distinguish a reference to a
periodical article from a reference to a chapter or pages in a book.
If you are in any doubt as to the nature of the reference (*i.e.*
whether it is a book, a periodical article or a law report) ask a
member of the library staff for advice. Articles written in
periodicals are not entered in the library catalogue under the names
of the authors.

1-8.   *Abbreviations*

One of the major difficulties facing a new student is the tradition,
adopted by lecturers and authors, of referring to periodicals and
law reports only by an abbreviated form of their title. Instead of
writing the name of the journal or law report in full they are
invariably shortened to such cryptic abbreviations as: [1975] A.C.;
[1974] 2 All E.R.; 127 N.L.J.; 4 L.M.C.L.Q. This may make it
very difficult for you to know whether you are looking for a law
report or a periodical article. Many of the references are confusingly
similar, *e.g.* L.R. can be the abbreviation for both "law report" and
"law review" (the law reports are shelved together, but separate
from law reviews which are periodicals, or journals). Consequently,
you could find yourself looking in the wrong sequence. A common
mistake is to assume that a reference to a report of a case in "Crim.
L.R." means that you must search amongst the law reports for a

series entitled the Criminal Law Reports. There is no such series (although there is a series called the *Criminal Appeal Reports*). The reference "Crim. L.R." is to the *Criminal Law Review*, which is a journal, shelved with the periodicals. This contains both articles and reports of cases.

You will find a list of abbreviations which are in common use, together with the full title of the journal or law report, in:

Where to Look for Your Law
Sweet & Maxwell's Guide to Law Reports and Statutes
The front pages of: the *Current Law Case Citator*; the *English and Empire Digest Cumulative Supplement*; the *Index to Legal Periodicals* and *Halsbury's Laws of England*, Volume 1
Manual of Legal Citations (published by the University of London Institute of Advanced Legal Studies)
Law Dictionaries, *e.g. Osborn's Concise Law Dictionary*.

A list of the most commonly used abbreviations is in Appendix 1 (p. 151) of this work.

1-9.   *Tracing Periodicals and Law Reports*

To find out if a periodical or law report is available look in the author catalogue, or in the separate periodicals catalogue, if there is one. The entry will indicate which volumes are available in the library and where they are shelved.

One point is especially worthy of note. Suppose that you are looking for a journal which includes the name of an organisation or body in its title, *e.g.* the *Journal of the Society of Public Teachers of Law*, or the *American Bar Association Journal*. If the publication you require is the bulletin, transactions, proceedings, journal, yearbook or annual report of an organisation, you may find in some libraries that the title has been reversed, so that the entry appears under the name of the organisation. For instance, in some libraries, the *Journal of the Society of Public Teachers of Law* would be entered under Society of Public Teachers of Law, whilst in others it appears under Journal.

If the journal or report you need is not available in your own library, the staff may be able to help you to locate a copy in another library in the area, or it may be possible to obtain the journal, or a photocopy, on interlibrary loan.

PROBLEMS

(a) Using the list of abbreviations at the front of the *Current Law Case Citator*, write down the full titles of the following:
W.L.R.
S.J.
New L.J.
M.L.R.
C.L.J.
All E.R.

Once you have discovered the full title, look up any three of these in the catalogues, and find the volumes on the shelves.

(b) Find the following periodical articles on your library shelves:
Barton, "The Rise of the Fee Simple" (1976) 92 L.Q.R. 108.
Ormrod, "Education and Training for the Professions" (1977) 30 C.L.P. 15.
Leigh, "Law Reform and the Law of Treason and Sedition" [1977] P.L. 128.

1-10.
WHICH LIBRARIES CAN I USE?

If you are studying at a university, polytechnic or college, the majority of the books you require should be available in your own institution's library. Remember that there may be more than one library available. For instance, in addition to the main library collection there may be a smaller collection of books and reports in your department or Faculty building. If you are living in a hall of residence, the hall's library may include some textbooks.

You may join the public library in the area in which you live, work or study. Most large towns will have some legal textbooks and law reports in their central library. If what you want is not available, the library staff may be able to borrow the material you require. This may take some time, so ask for the material well in advance of your actual need.

Should you return home for the vacation, the university or

polytechnic nearest your home may allow you to use their library for reference. Your own library staff can give you advice and provide you with the addresses and opening hours of libraries.

If you are studying for a professional examination, your professional body will have a library, from which you may be able to borrow books (by post, if necessary). The nearest large public library is another possible source of supply, and your employer may have a library to which you can have access.

Students studying for the Bar may use the library of their Inn. Local public libraries, the libraries attached to the courts, and the collections available in chambers are other possible sources. Those training to be solicitors can use the facilities of the Law Society's library, and the collections held by local law societies may be made available to students. External students of London University may borrow books by post but for law reports they may have to rely on access to a public library. If students are in difficulties they should approach the librarian of the nearest institution which has a law collection and explain their circumstances. Most libraries are willing to provide some assistance to students in genuine need.

The addresses of libraries can be found in the Library Association's *Libraries in the United Kingdom and the Republic of Ireland*, or the information can be obtained, by telephone or in person, from any public library. A more detailed guide is B. Mangles, *Directory of Law Libraries in the British Isles*.

1-11.   ASSISTANCE FROM LIBRARY STAFF

Remember that the library staff are there to help you. They will be pleased to explain how the books are arranged on the shelves, to decipher abbreviations, help with difficulties with reading lists and suggest possible sources of information. Do not hesitate to ask them for advice, no matter how busy they may appear to be. Never be afraid that your enquiry is too trivial or that you will appear foolish or ignorant by asking for advice. Most libraries produce handouts or library guides, which are usually available free. You should make a point of obtaining (and reading) those which are relevant. They will explain how the books are arranged on the shelves, how to use the catalogues, how to borrow books, etc. In academic libraries, tours of the library are often arranged at the beginning of the session. If such a tour is available you should certainly attend, as it will help you to familiarise yourself with the library.

PROBLEMS

You may find it useful to find out the answers to the following questions about the library which you will be using most frequently.

(a) How many books can I borrow at one time? How long can I keep them on loan?

(b) Is there a separate collection of books in very heavy demand? If so, where is it? How long can I keep the books from this collection?

(c) Can I borrow periodicals? If so, for how long?

(d) Is there a coin-operated photocopying machine available, so that I can make copies of articles, reports, etc.? How much does each copy cost?

(e) Is change for the photocopying machine available in the library?

(f) Is there a separate collection of government publications? If so, where is it?

(g) Is there a separate catalogue of periodicals and law reports?

(h) Have you located the nearest toilets, refreshment rooms, smoking areas?

(i) Should I reshelve books and law reports after use or leave them on the tables?

(j) Are the law reports from *The Times* available in the library?

1-12.   DICTIONARIES AND DIRECTORIES

The newcomer to law rapidly discovers that lawyers have a language of their own, which is a mixture of Latin, French and English. There are several small pocket dictionaries of legal terms which are useful for students, *e.g.* P. G. Osborn, *Concise Law Dictionary* (6th ed.) and Mozley and Whiteley, *Law Dictionary* (9th ed.). Students should also consult standard English dictionaries, such as the great *Oxford English Dictionary* or one of its smaller versions. W. A. Jowitt, *Dictionary of English Law* (2nd ed.) is a larger legal dictionary. Latin phrases and maxims may cause difficulties for students who have no classical languages. Sweet and Maxwell publish a book entitled *Latin for Lawyers*, which includes many Latin phrases. Latin phrases also appear in most legal dictionaries. A collection of legal maxims will be found in H. Broom, *A Selection of Legal Maxims* (10th ed.).

A list of all practising solicitors and barristers in this country in 1976, together with addresses of courts, and a list of court officials, judges, etc., is to be found in *The Law List 1976*. This was formerly published annually, but the 1976 list was the last to appear. It has been replaced by two separate works: *The Bar List of the United Kingdom* and the *Solicitors' Diary and Directory*.

Chapter 2

LAW REPORTS

2-1.   INTRODUCTION

A basic or primary source of English law is the information found
in the law reports. Traditionally the common law has developed
through the practical reasoning of the judges which is based on the
particular facts of the case in question, social forces, and also upon
previous judicial reasoning when it has a bearing on the case being
heard. Legal principles stated in earlier decisions are given effect in
later cases by the operation of the doctrine of precedent, which is
described in detail in Glanville Williams, *Learning the Law*, Chap.
6. The successful development of the common law depends largely
upon the production of reliable law reports which carry not only
the facts, issues and decision but also, and most importantly, the
legal principles upon which the judgment is made. Increasingly,
the judiciary have been called upon to consider the scope and
application of particular Acts of Parliament. Important cases which
provide the opportunity for judicial consideration of such Acts also
find their way into the law reports. It is not possible to report
every case that is heard, nor is such a task necessary. A case is
selected for reporting if it raises a point of legal significance or
importance. On the basis of such reporting, judges, to a greater or
lesser extent, follow or are influenced by their own previous
decisions and those of colleagues and predecessors. Throughout
your legal training and practice you will make constant use of these
reports. Hence, a thorough working knowledge of them is
essential. Glanville Williams (*Learning the Law*, 10th ed., p. 28)
has offered the following advice to students of law:

> "The great disadvantage of confining oneself to textbooks and
> lecture notes is that it means taking all one's law at second
> hand. The law of England is contained in statutes and judicial
> decisions; what the text writer thinks is not, in itself, law. He
> may have misinterpreted the authorities, and the reader who
> goes to them goes to the fountainhead. Besides familiarising

himself with the law reports and statute book, the lawyer-to-be should get to know his way about the library as a whole, together with its apparatus of catalogues and books of reference."

2-2.   EARLY LAW REPORTS

Law reports have existed, in one form or another, since the reign of Edward I. These very early law reports are known as the **Year Books**. If you wish to see a copy, a number of these *Year Books* have been reprinted in the series of publications published by the Selden Society, or in the **Rolls Series** (both of which will usually be found in the history section of a general library.)

The *Year Books* were replaced by reports published privately by individuals, and these reports are normally referred to by the name of the author or compiler of the reports. For this reason they are collectively referred to as the **Nominate Reports**. They vary considerably in accuracy and reliability (Williams, *Learning the Law*, 10th ed., p. 30). Few libraries will have a complete collection of these old reports and, if you do obtain a copy, you may find that the antiquated print makes it difficult to read. Fortunately, the great majority of these Nominate Reports have been reprinted in a series called the **English Reports**, which we shall examine in detail later (para. 2-10).

2-3.   MODERN LAW REPORTS

In 1865, a body called the Incorporated Council of Law Reporting commenced publication of a series entitled the **Law Reports**. These reports, which are semi-official, were rapidly accepted by the legal profession as the most authoritative version of law reports and most of the privately published series ceased publication in 1865, or soon after that date. The *Law Reports* have maintained their superiority and today it is the report which appears in the *Law Reports* which is preferably cited (quoted) in courts. At the present time the *All England Law Reports* is the only general series of law reports which is still privately published. However, there are a number of specialist law reports, *e.g.* the **Criminal Appeal Reports**, and the **Road Traffic Reports**, which are produced by commercial publishers.

A report of a case may appear in more than one series of reports. For instance, a report may appear in **The Times** newspaper, (under the heading "Law Report") the day after the case is heard. A week or two later the case may be published in one or both of the two general series of law reports which appear weekly; the **All England Law Reports** and the **Weekly Law Reports**. At about the same time a summary, or a full report, may be published in some of the weekly legal journals, such as the **New Law Journal** and the **Solicitors' Journal**, or in specialist law reports and journals (*e.g.* **Tax Cases**, the **Criminal Law Review**). Some time later a final, authoritative version (which has been personally checked by the judges concerned) will be published in the *Law Reports*. Thus you may be given, or you may find, references to more than one report of a case.

2-4.   *Citation and Format of Law Reports*

Law teachers, and writers of textbooks, often use a number of abbreviations when referring to the sources where a report of a case can be found. These can appear very confusing at first, but constant use will rapidly make you familiar with the meaning of most of the abbreviations used. A reference to a case (which is called a citation) will normally look similar to the following example:

Halden[1] v. *Halden*[1] [1966][2] W.L.R.[3] 1481[4]

[1]the names of the parties involved in the case;
[2]the year in which the case is reported;
[3]the name of the series of law reports in which the report of the case appears. (The name of the series is often abbreviated.) If there are several volumes containing the cases for that year, the volume which contains the case you require is indicated;
[4]the page number at which the case commences.

Thus in this example, the case *Halden* v. *Halden* will be found in the 1966 volumes of the *Weekly Law Reports* (abbreviated to W.L.R. — for details of how to find the meaning of abbreviations see para. 2-12). There are, in fact, three volumes of the *Weekly Law Reports* containing the cases reported in 1966. The case referred to will be found in the first volume, at page 1481.

Let us look now at a typical specimen of a law report. (Illustration I)

A

CLEVELAND PETROLEUM CO., LTD. *v.* DARTSTONE, LTD. AND ANOTHER. (1)

[COURT OF APPEAL, CIVIL DIVISION—Lord Denning, M.R., Russell and Salmon, L.JJ.), November 26, 1968.] (2)

B   *Trade—Restraint of trade—Agreement—Petrol filling station—Solus agreement—Lease by garage owner to petrol supplier—Underlease to company to operate service station—Covenant in underlease for exclusive sale of supplier's products—Assignment of underlease by licence granted by supplier—Interim injunction to restrain breach of covenant.* (3)

S. the owner in fee simple of a garage, leased the premises to the plaintiffs
C   for 25 years from 1st July 1960. The plaintiffs granted an underlease to C.O.S.S.,Ltd., by which C.O.S.S., Ltd., covenanted, inter alia, to carry on the business of a petrol filling station at all times and not to sell or distribute motor fuels other than those supplied by the plaintiffs. After several assignments the underlease was assigned to the defendants who undertook to observe and perform the covenants. The defendants thereupon challenged
D   the validity of the ties. The plaintiffs issued a writ claiming an injunction restraining the defendants from breaking this covenant. The plaintiffs obtained an interim injunction against which the defendants appealed. (4)

Held: the appeal would be dismissed, the tie was valid and not an unreasonable restraint of trade because the defendants, not having been in possession previously, took possession of the premises under a lease and
E   entered into a restrictive covenant knowing about such covenant, and thereby bound themselves to it (see p. 203, letters C, F and G, post).

Dicta in *Esso Petroleum Co., Ltd.* v. *Harper's Garage (Stourport), Ltd.* ([1967] 1 All E.R. at pp. 707, 714, and 724, 725) applied.

Appeal dismissed. (5)

F   [As to agreements in restraint of trade, see 38 HALSBURY'S LAWS (3rd Edn.) 20, para. 13; and for cases on the subject, see 45 DIGEST (Repl.) 443-449, 271-297.] (6)

Case referred to:
Esso Petroleum Co., Ltd. v. *Harper's Garage (Stourport), Ltd.*, [1967] 1 All E.R. 699; [1968] A.C. 269; [1967] 2 W.L.R. 871; Digest (Repl.) Supp. (7)
G

Interlocutory Appeal.
This was an appeal by the defendants, Dartstone, Ltd., and James Arthur Gregory, from an order of EVELEIGH, J., dated 1st November 1968, granting an interim injunction restraining the defendants from acting in breach of a covenant contained in an underlease made on 1st July 1960 between the plaintiffs, Cleve-
H   land Petroleum Co., Ltd., and County Oak Service Station, Ltd., and assigned to the defendants on 30th August 1968. The facts are set out in the judgment of LORD DENNING, M.R. (8)

Raymond Walton, Q.C., and *M. C. B. Buckley* for the defendants. (9)
A. P. Leggatt for the plaintiffs. (10)

I   LORD DENNING, M.R.: This case concerns a garage and petrol station called County Oak service station, at Crawley in Sussex. Mr. Sainsbury was the owner in fee simple. On 1st July 1960, there were three separate transactions: First, Mr. Sainsbury granted a lease of the entire premises to the plaintiffs, Cleveland Petroleum Co., Ltd., for 25 years, from 1st July 1960. The plaintiffs paid him £50,000 premium and agreed also to pay a nominal rent of £10 a year. Secondly, the plaintiffs granted an underlease of the premises to a company called County Oak Service Station, Ltd. That company was one in which Mr. Sainsbury had a predominant interest. The underlease was for 25 years, less three days from

Illustration I

The citation is *Cleveland Petroleum Co. Ltd.* v. *Dartstone Ltd.* [1969] 1 All E.R. 201. Several key points in the illustration are numbered.

1   The names of the parties. In a civil case the name of the plaintiff (the person bringing the action) comes first, followed by the name of the defendant. A criminal case is usually cited as *R.* v. *Smith*. R. is the abbreviated form for the Latin words "Rex" (King) or "Regina" (Queen). The charge against Smith, the accused in a criminal offence, is brought on behalf of the Crown. The small letter "v." between the names of the parties to the action is an abbreviation of the Latin "versus" (against). When speaking of a case you say "against" in criminal cases, or "and" in civil cases, but never "v." or "versus." (Williams, *Learning the Law*, 10th ed., pp. 13 *et seq.*)

2   The name of the court in which the case was heard, the names of the judges (M.R.: Master of the Rolls; L.JJ.: Lords Justices) and the date on which the case was heard.

3   A summary (in italics) of the main legal issues of the case. You are advised not to rely upon this as it is neither necessarily complete nor accurate.

4   The headnote, which is a brief statement of the case, and the nature of the claim (in a civil case) or a charge (in a criminal case).

5   The court's ruling is stated, with a summary of reasons.

6   In certain reports, *e.g.* *All England Law Reports*, the major legal points are cross-referenced to *Halsbury's Laws* and the *English and Empire Digest*.

7   A list of cases which were referred to during the hearing.

8   This is an appeal against the decision of a lower court to grant an interim or interlocutory injunction. An injunction is an order given by a judge telling a party to do something or refrain from doing it. It is interim or interlocutory in that it is temporary and meant to preserve the status quo before the legal rights are fully considered in court at a later date.

9   The names of counsel who appeared for the parties (Q.C.: Queen's Counsel).

10   The judgment of Lord Denning, M.R.

2-5. *Format of Recent Unbound Reports*

Because the law is constantly changing, with new cases being reported every week, you will often be asked to consult recent cases and these can present some difficulties. A reference to a report which appeared in *The Times* newspaper may be available in your library in one of several forms. The library may keep the daily copies of *The Times* (perhaps bound up into large volumes), or they may have replaced these by photographing the pages onto a reel of film, known as a microfilm. If *The Times* is available on microfilm the library staff will show you how to operate the machine which is needed to consult the film. Depending upon the equipment available, they may be able to make a full-size photocopy of relevant items for you. Another possibility is that a law librarian may have cut out of the newspaper all the law reports and filed them in folders. Ask the library staff if the law reports from *The Times* are available in your library and where they are kept.

If you are referred to a report of a case in the *All England Law Reports*, or the *Weekly Law Reports* (or, indeed, most other series of law reports) which has been published during the last few months, you will not find a bound volume on the shelves but a series of papercovered parts, or issues. However, your reference (citation) will make it appear that you are looking for a bound volume. So how do you find it? If you examine one of the weekly issues of the **All England Law Reports** you will find, at the top of the front cover, the date of that issue, the part (or issue) number, and the year, volume and page numbers covered by that issue. For example:

24th January 1978   Part 4   [1978] 1 All ER 225 – 304

This indicates that this issue (Part 4), will eventually form pages 225 – 304 of the first bound volume of the *All England Law Reports* for 1978. Also on the front cover appears a list of all the cases reported in that part, showing the page number on which each report begins.

Many other law reports also issue a number of parts during the current year. At the end of the year these are replaced by a bound volume or volumes and, in every case, the part will indicate on its cover the volume and pages in the bound volume where it will later appear. The **Weekly Law Reports** is a series (which commenced in 1953) that you will consult frequently. The arrangement of its weekly issues is rather confusing. Three bound volumes are produced each year, and each weekly issue contains some cases which will eventually appear in Volume 1 of the bound volumes for that year, and some cases which will subsequently appear in either Volume 2 or Volume 3. On the front cover of each issue the contents of that part, and which volumes the pages in that issue will eventually appear in, are shown. For example:

Part 8 March 3 1978
[1978] 1 W.L.R. 265–301
[1978] 2 W.L.R. 473–499

Part 8 therefore contains pages 265–301 of what will eventually form the first volume of the *Weekly Law Reports* for 1978, and pages 473–499 of the second volume. (A sheet of green paper is inserted in the issue to mark the division between the pages destined for Volume 1 and those forming part of Volume 2.) A list of all the cases included in the part is printed on the front cover, and the volume and page number for each case is shown. You many wonder why the publishers (the Incorporated Council of Law Reporting, who also publish the **Law Reports**) have chosen this method of publishing the issues. The reason is that the cases in Volume 1 (which are less significant), will not appear in the *Law Reports*, whilst those which appear in Volumes 2 and 3 will be republished in the *Law Reports*.

You will probably find that the latest copy of law reports (and journals) will be displayed in a separate area of the library. The remainder of the issues for the current year may also be filed in this area or they may be in a box on the shelves alongside the bound volumes.

2-6.   *The Law Reports*

The publication known as the **Law Reports** was first issued in 1865. It was originally published in 11 series, each covering different courts. The rationalisation of the court structure since that time has reduced this to four series. These are:

Appeal Cases (abbreviated to A.C.)
Chancery Division (Ch.)
Queen's Bench Division (Q.B.)
Family Division (Fam.)

You will normally find that the *Law Reports* are arranged on the shelves in this order.

2-7. HOW THE LAW REPORTS ARE ARRANGED ON THE SHELVES

The physical location of the various earlier series reflects their relationship to the present four series. For example, the historical predecessors of the present **Queen's Bench Division** (called the **King's Bench Division** when a King is on the throne) were the **Court for Crown Cases Reserved**, the **Court of Common Pleas** and the **Court of Exchequer**. These are therefore shelved before the Queen's Bench Division reports (because they are its predecessors) but after the **Appeal Cases** and **Chancery Division** reports. The same arrangement is applied with the other three current series (*i.e.* the predecessors of the present courts are filed at the beginning of each series).

Table 1 (p. 20) shows the way in which the *Law Reports* will be found to be arranged on the shelves in most libraries. The abbreviations used to denote each series are shown, and also the dates during which each series appeared.

Table I: (Reproduced From G. Williams, *Learning the Law* (10th ed.), p. 34)

TABLE OF THE LAW REPORTS

The mode of citation is given in brackets. In the first, second and third columns, dots (...) are put where the number of the volume would appear in the citation. In the fourth column square brackets ([ ]) are put where the year would appear in the citation.

1866–1875	1875–1880	1881–1890	1891–present
House of Lords, English and Irish Appeals (L.R. ... H.L.) House of Lords, Scotch and Divorce Appeals (L.R. ... H.L.Sc. or L.R. ... H.L.Sc. and Div.) Privy Council Appeals (L.R. ... P.C.)	Appeal Cases (...App.Cas.)	Appeal Cases (...App.Cas.)	Appeal Cases ([ ] A.C.)
Chancery Appeal Cases (L.R. ... Ch. or Ch. App.) Equity Cases (L.R. ... Eq.)	Chancery Division (...Ch.D.)	Chancery Division (...Ch.D.)	Chancery Division ([ ] Ch.)
Crown Cases Reserved (L.R. ... C.C., or, ... C.C.R.) Queen's Bench Cases * (L.R. ... Q.B.) Common Pleas Cases (L.R. ... C.P.) Exchequer Cases ‡ (L.R. ... Ex.)	Queen's Bench Division (...Q.B.D.) Common Pleas Division (...C.P.D.) Exchequer Division (...Ex.D.)	Queen's Bench Division (...Q.B.D.)	Queen's (or King's Bench Division ([ ] Q.B. or K.B.) †
Admiralty and Ecclesiastical Cases (L.R. ... A. & E.) Probate and Divorce Cases (L.R. ... P. & D.)	Probate Division (...P.D.)	Probate Division (...P.D.)	Probate Division ([ ] P.) Since 1972 Family Division ([ ] Fam.)

* Note that there is also a series called Queen's Bench Reports in the old reports (113–118 E.R.).
† After 1907 this includes cases in the Court of Criminal Appeal, later the Court of Appeal, in place of the previous Court for Crown Cases Reserved.
‡ Note that there is also a series called Exchequer Reports in the old reports (154–156 E.R.).

2-8.   CITATION OF THE LAW REPORTS

You may notice that in some cases the date is printed in square brackets, whilst in other cases it is enclosed within round brackets. There are certain conventions concerning the way in which the citations (references) to cases in the **Law Reports** are written and these must be mastered.

Until 1890 each volume in the various series had its own individual number and these numbers ran on from year to year. Thus the 10 volumes of *Exchequer Cases* published between 1865 and 1875 were individually numbered, 1 to 10, and it is the volume number rather than the year which is important in locating the correct volume. To show that the date is not essential, but is merely an aid, it is placed within round brackets, *e.g. Harrop* v. *Hirst* (1868-69) L.R. 4 Ex. 43. The abbreviation L.R. (for *Law Reports*) has been omitted from the citation for all series since 1875. The one exception to this was a series, published from 1957 to 1972, entitled **Reports of Restrictive Practices** cases. This was published by the Incorporated Council of Law Reporting and the citation took the form L.R. . . . R.P. In many libraries you will find that it is shelved separately from the *Law Reports*.

Since 1891, the individual numbering of volumes has been discontinued, except when there is more than one volume published in any particular year. When this happens the volumes within the year are numbered to distinguish them, as is done with the **Weekly Law Reports**, and the **All England Law Reports**. The main arrangement within each series since 1891 has been by date. To indicate that the date is essential if you are to trace the report it is placed within square brackets, *e.g. Att.-Gen.* v. *Times Newspapers* [1974] A.C. 273. This convention of using round and square brackets is also used in other series such as the *All England Law Reports*. The use of brackets may be summarised as follows:

Date in round brackets: the date is not of major importance, but the volume number is: *e.g.* (1868) L.R.6 Eq. 540.

Date in square brackets: the date is an essential part of the reference, *e.g.* [1895] A.C. 229; [1954] 3 W.L.R. 967; [1953] 2 All E.R. 608.

SUMMARY: CONVENTIONS GOVERNING THE CORRECT CITATION OF THE LAW REPORTS

1865–1875: (year) L.R. volume, abbreviation for series, page; *e.g. Rylands* v. *Fletcher* (1868) L.R. 3 H.L. 330.

1875–1890: (year) volume, abbreviation for series (L.R. is omitted), page; *e.g. Brogden* v. *Metropolitan Railway Co.* (1877) 2 App.Cas. 666.

1891–date: [year] volume within year, abbreviation for series, page; *e.g. Carlill* v. *Carbolic Smoke Ball Co.* [1892] 2 Q.B. 484.

It is worth noting that the abbreviation H.L. (see the citation for *Rylands* v. *Fletcher*, above) does not stand for a series entitled Law Reports: House of Lords. It is the abbreviation for a series entitled **Law Reports: English and Irish Appeal Cases**, which you will find shelved at the beginning of the Appeal Cases sequence (see Table 1, p. 20).

PROBLEMS

(a) Place the appropriate brackets around the date, and include volume number if required, in the following citations.
Plomley v. *Felton* 1889 App. Cas.61;
Macedo v. *Stroud* 1922 A.C.330;
Morris v. *Luton Corporation* 1946 K.B.114;

(b) Are the following citations correct? If not, correct the errors:
Goddard v. *Jones* (1872–75) L.R. 3 P. & D. 8.
Cave v. *Hastings* (1881) 7 Q.B.D. 125.
Horam v. *Hayhoe* (1904) 1 K.B. 289.

2-9   OLDER LAW REPORTS

We have concentrated upon the modern series of law reports because these are the reports which you will be using most frequently. However, from time to time you will need to look at older cases, that is, those reported in the first half of the nineteenth century, or even several centuries earlier. Reports of older cases can be found in several series: the **English Reports, Revised Reports, Law Journal Reports, Law Times Reports** and the **All England Law Reports Reprint** series. We shall now look at some of these series in more detail.

We have said that the reports published privately by individuals (and known as the *Nominate Reports*) ceased publication around 1865, when the *Law Reports* were first published. Thus the date 1865 is an important one for you to remember. If the date of the case you want is before 1865 you are most likely to find it in a series known as the *English Reports*. If this series is not available in your library, you may need to use the *Revised Reports*, which is similar but not identical in its coverage.

2-10.   *How to use the English Reports*

If you know the name of the case, look it up in the alphabetical index of the names of cases, printed in Volumes 177–178 of the **English Reports**. Beside the name of the case is printed the abbreviation for the name of the original nominate reporter, and the volume and page in his reports where the case appeared. The number printed in **bold** type adjoining this is the volume number in the **English Reports** where the case will be found, and this is followed by the page number in that volume, (Illustration II, p. 24):

Daniel v. *North*[a] 11 East, 372[b] 103[c] 1047[d];

[a]name of the case;

[b]volume, name of original reporter, page number in original report, *i.e.* original report appeared in Volume 11 of *East's Reports* at page 372;

[c]reprint of report appears in *English Reports*, Vol. 103, page 1047.

You will see that Volume 103 of the **English Reports** has the volumes and names of the *Nominate Reports* which are to be found in that volume printed on the spine. Page number 1047 appears in its normal position at the top outer corner of the page whilst the volume and page number of the original report are printed at the inner margin. This can sometimes cause confusion to new students. (See Illustration III, p. 25.)

424 **DAN** INDEX OF CASES

Daniel *v.* North, 11 East, 372	**103** 1047
—— *v.* Phillips, 4 T. R. 499	**100** 1141
—— *v.* Pit, Peake Add. Cas. 238	**170** 257
—— *v.* Pit, 6 Esp. 74	**170** 834
—— *v.* Purbeck, W. Kel. 97	**25** 510
—— *v.* Purkis, W. Kel. 97	**25** 510
—— *v.* Purkurst, 2 Barn. K. B. 214, 220	**94** 457, 461
—— *v.* Russell, 14 Ves. Jun. 393 ; 2 Ves. Jun. Supp. 376	**33** 572 ; **34** 1139
—— *v.* Skipwith, 2 Bro. C. C. 155	**29** 89
—— *v.* Sterlin, 1 Freeman, 50	**89** 39
—— *v.* Thompson, 15 East, 78	**104** 774
—— *v.* Trotman, 1 Moo. N. S. 123	**15** 649
—— *v.* Turpin, 1 Keble, 124	**83** 852
—— *v.* Ubley, Jones, W. 137	**82** 73
—— *v.* Uply, Latch, 9, 39, 134	**82** 248, 264, 312
—— *v.* Upton, Noy, 80	**74** 1047
—— *v.* Waddington, Cro. Jac. 377	**79** 322
—— *v.* Waddington, 3 Bulstrode, 130	**81** 111
—— *v.* Warren, 2 Y. & C. C. C. 290	**63** 127
—— *v.* Wilkin, 7 Ex. 429	**155** 1016
—— *v.* Wilkin, 8 Ex. 156	**155** 1300
—— *v.* Wilson, 5 T. R. 1	**101** 1
Daniel's Case, 2 Dy. 133 b	**73** 291
—— Trust, *In re*, 18 Beav. 309	**52** 122

Illustration II: EXTRACT FROM INDEX OF CASES IN THE ENGLISH REPORTS

before ; but they could not agree on the person to be substituted, and therefore the original appointment stood as before.
Per Curiam. Rule absolute.

AMBROSE *against* REES. Wednesday, June 14th, 1809. Notice having been given for the trial of a cause at Monmouth, which arose in Glamorganshire, as being in fact the next English county since the st. 27 H. 8, c. 26, s. 4, though Hereford be the common place of trial ; the Court refused to set aside the verdict as for a mis-trial, on motion ; the question being open on the record.

Marryat opposed a rule for setting aside the verdict obtained in this cause, upon the ground of an irregularity in the trial. The venue was laid in Glamorganshire, and the cause was tried at Monmouth, as the next English county where the King's writ of venire runs(*b*) ; but it was objected that it ought to have been tried at Hereford, according to the general custom that all causes in which the venue is laid in any county in South Wales should be tried at Hereford. But the rule being that the cause should be tried in the next English county, and Monmouth being in fact the next English county to Glamorganshire, and more conveniently situated for the trial of the cause, there seems no solid ground for impeaching the validity of the trial ; though the practice relied on is easily accounted for by the consideration that Monmouthshire was originally a Welch county, and till it became an English county in the 27th year of Hen. 8, Herefordshire was in fact the next English county to Glamorgan. And there is no reason for setting aside this verdict on the ground of surprize ; for the defendant had not merely a notice of trial in the next English county, generally, which might have misled him by the notoriety of the [371] practice, but a specific notice of trial at Monmouth, to which he made no objection at the time.

Abbott, in support of the rule, relied on the known practice which had always prevailed, as well since as before the Statute 27 H. 8 ; and referred to *Morgan* v. *Morgan* (*a*), where the question arose in 1656, upon an ejectment for lands in Breknock-shire, which was tried at Monmouth ; and afterwards judgment was arrested, on the ground of a mis-trial, as it ought to have been tried in Herefordshire ; for that Monmouthshire was but made an English county by statute within time of memory ; and that trials in the next English county of issues arising in Wales have been time out of mind and at the common law ; so that a place newly made an English county cannot have such a trial. And he observed, that if this trial were good, all the judgments in causes out of Glamorganshire tried at Hereford have been erroneous.

Lord Ellenborough C.J. If the question appear on the record, then the defendant cannot apply in this summary manner. And as he did not object at the time, we shall not relieve him upon motion.
Per Curiam. Rule discharged.

[372] DANIEL *against* NORTH. Wednesday, June 14th, 1809. Where lights had been put out and enjoyed without interruption for above 20 years during the occupation of the opposite premises by a tenant ; that will not conclude the landlord of such opposite premises, without evidence of his knowledge of the fact, which is the foundation of presuming a grant against him ; and consequently will not conclude a succeeding tenant who was in possession under such landlord from building up against such encroaching lights.

[Considered and applied, *Wheaton* v. *Maple* [1893], 3 Ch. 57 ; *Roberts* v. *James*, 1903, 89 L. T. 286. For ·*Rugby Charity* v. *Merryweather*, 11 East, 375, n., see *Woodyer* v. *Hadden*, 1813, 5 Taunt. 138 ; *Wood* v. *Veal*, 1822, 5 B. & Ald. 457 ; *Vernon* v. *St. James's, Westminster*, 1880, 16 Ch. D. 457 ; *Bourke* v. *Davis*, 1889, 44 Ch. D. 123.]

The plaintiff declared in case, upon his seisin in fee of a certain messuage or dwelling-house in Stockport, on one side of which there is and was and of right ought to be six windows ; and stated that the defendant wrongfully erected a wall 60 feet high and 50 in length near the said house and windows, and obstructed the light and

_____

(*b*) Vide 1 Term Rep. 313.   (*a*) Hard. 66.

Illustration III : PAGE OF ENGLISH REPORTS

You may have only a citation (reference) to the original **Nominate Report,** *e.g.* 3 Car. & P. (*Carrington and Payne*), 2 Barn. & Ald. (*Barnewall and Alderson*) or 3 M. & W. This reference is usually printed only in an abbreviated form. The first problem, therefore, is to discover the reporter's full name. This can be done by looking up the abbreviation in *Sweet & Maxwell's Guide to Law Reports and Statutes* or some other list of abbreviations (para. 2-12), or in the **Chart to the English Reports.** From these you will find that the abbreviation 3 M. & W. is a reference to *Meeson and Welsby's Exchequer Rep rts.* Next turn to the *Chart to the English Reports.* This may be displayed near the **English Reports,** or it may be a slim volume shelved with the Reports. Looking under "M" you find that *Meeson and Welsby* is reprinted in Volumes 150–153 of the **English Reports.** On the outside of these four volumes the contents of each are printed. This indicates that Volumes 1 to 4 of *Meeson and Welsby* are reprinted in Volume 150 of the **English Reports.** Inside the volume, at the top inner margin, is printed the volume and page number of the original report. The numbers in square brackets, in the text of the reports, indicate when the page numbers of the original report changed.

PROBLEMS

(a) Using the Index volumes (Vols. 177–178) complete the following citations and state the volume and page in the *English Reports* where the case will be found:

Lens v. *Brown*

Garter v. *Dee*

Bourman v. *Wild*

ALGORITHM DESIGNED TO SHOW HOW TO LOOK UP A CASE IN THE ENGLISH REPORTS

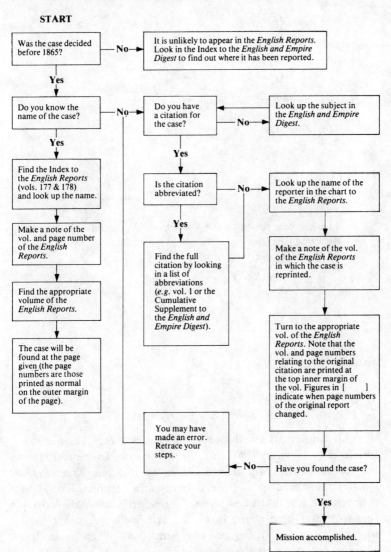

START

Was the case decided before 1865?

— No→ It is unlikely to appear in the *English Reports*. Look in the Index to the *English and Empire Digest* to find out where it has been reported.

Yes

Do you know the name of the case?

— No→ Do you have a citation for the case?

← Look up the subject in the *English and Empire Digest*. — No—

Yes

Find the Index to the *English Reports* (vols. 177 & 178) and look up the name.

Yes

Is the citation abbreviated? — No→ Look up the name of the reporter in the chart to the *English Reports*.

Make a note of the vol. and page number of the *English Reports*.

Yes

Find the appropriate volume of the *English Reports*.

Find the full citation by looking in a list of abbreviations (*e.g.* vol. 1 or the Cumulative Supplement to the *English and Empire Digest*).

Make a note of the vol. of the *English Reports* in which the case is reprinted.

The case will be found at the page given (the page numbers are those printed as normal on the outer margin of the page).

Turn to the appropriate vol. of the *English Reports*. Note that the vol. and page numbers relating to the original citation are printed at the top inner margin of the vol. Figures in [   ] indicate when page numbers of the original report changed.

You may have made an error. Retrace your steps.

← No— Have you found the case?

Yes

Mission accomplished.

(b) Name the cases reported in the following *Nominate Reports* and give the volume and page in the *English Reports* where they appear:
2 Atk. 77
7 H. & N. 56
6 B. & C. 23

(c) Give the full title of the following abbreviations:
Giff.
Moo. P.C.N.S.
T.R.

(d) In what volumes of the *English Reports* do the following *Nominate Reports* appear?
12 Vesey, Junior
6 Modern
1 El. & Bl.

2-11.   *Other Older Law Reports*

The **All England Law Reports Reprint** is another useful source for old cases between 1558 and 1935. The cases are reprinted from the reports which originally appeared in the *Law Times Reports,* which commenced in 1843, and from earlier reports. The *Reprint* contains some 5,000 cases selected principally upon the criterion that they have been referred to in the *All England Law Reports* and in *Halsbury's Laws of England* (see para. 6-3). There is an Index volume containing an alphabetical list of cases and a subject index of the cases included in the reprint.

Two other series of nineteenth century cases are also referred to: the *Law Journal Reports* and the *Law Times Reports*. The **Law Journal Reports** cover the period 1822–1949. They can be complicated to use because usually two volumes were published each year, both bearing the same numbers. In one were printed the cases heard in common law courts, while the other printed equity cases. It is therefore necessary to decide whether the case you want is likely to appear in the common law or the equity volume for that year, or you will need to check both volumes. To add to the difficulty, the volume numbering and the method of citation changed during the course of its publication. The first nine volumes (1822–1831) are known as the old series (L.J.O.S.). References to the new series (1832–1949) omit the letters N.S. Citations give the abbreviation for the court in which the case was heard. It is therefore necessary to decide if the court was a court of common law or equity, so that you consult the correct volume. For example, the reference 16 L.J.Q.B. 274 is a reference to the *Law Journal (New Series)*, Volume 16 in the common law volume (since Queen's Bench was a court of common law) at page 274 of the reports of Queen's Bench. Each court's reports are paginated separately.

The **Law Times Reports** (L.T.) cover the period 1859–1947. Prior to this, the reports were published as part of the journal entitled *Law Times* and these are cited as the *Law Times, Old Series* (L.T.O.S.) which ran from 1843–1860. You may find this Old Series is shelved with the journals, not with the law reports.

PROBLEMS

(a) Complete the citation to the following cases in the *All England Law Reports Reprint:*
Mills v. *Jones*
Streatfield v. *Streatfield*
What case has been reported on the subject of a Restaurant Keeper?

(b) What case is found at:
79 L.J.K.B. 241
106 L.J.Ch. 36
15 L.J.Ch. 73

2-12.   HOW TO FIND THE MEANING OF ABBREVIATIONS

If you are faced with an abbreviation for a law report (or journal) which you do not recognise, you can find the full title of the report by looking in any of the following works:

Sweet & Maxwell's Guide to Law Reports and Statutes;
Where to Look for Your Law;
Current Law Citators;
English and Empire Digest (Vol. 1 and the Cumulative Supplement);
Halsbury's Laws of England (4th ed., Vol. 1, pp. 23–48);
Halsbury's Laws of England (3rd ed., Vol. 1, pp. [31–53]);
Osborn's Concise Law Dictionary;
Manual of Legal Citations (Pts. I and II, published by the University of London Institute of Advanced Legal Studies).

If you are unable to find the abbreviation in any of these books, ask a member of the library staff for help. Once you know the full title of the report, check in the library's catalogue or in its list of periodicals and reports (para. 1-9) to see if that series is available in the library, and where it is shelved. A list of some of the most commonly used abbreviations will be found in Appendix 1 to this book (pp. 151–156).

2-13.   HOW TO FIND A CASE WHEN YOU ONLY KNOW THE NAME

We will now turn to some of the problems frequently encountered by students and attempt to show how these can be answered.

It is a common difficulty to find that you know the name of a case but you have no note of where the case was reported; or else the reference which you have been given has proved to be inaccurate. How can you find out where a report of the case appears?

The easiest way of tracing a case of any date is to look it up in the *Current Law Citators*. If you fail to find it there you should turn to other sources such as the *English and Empire Digest* or the indexes to specific series of law reports, such as the *Law Reports*.

2-14.   *How to Use the* Current Law Case Citator *and the*
            Current Law Citator

The **Current Law Case Citator** contains an alphabetical list of
cases of any date which have been published, or quoted in court,
between 1947 and 1976. There were two versions published; one
was entitled the **Scottish Current Law Case Citator**, the other
was simply called the **Current Law Case Citator.** If your library
has the Scottish version, do not think that it is of no use to you
because you are looking for an English case. Despite the name, the
Scottish Current Law Case Citator does contain all the English
cases, plus Scottish cases (which are omitted from the other
edition). The Scottish cases form a separate alphabetical sequence at
the back of the volume. The information is kept up to date by the
Current Law Citator, which is published annually. It contains
details of cases of any date which have been published or quoted in
court since 1977. The **Current Law Case Citator** and **Current
Law Citator** should, therefore, be used together.

The cases are listed in alphabetical order. Cases beginning
simply with a letter of the alphabet, *e.g. S.* v. *C.* are at the
beginning of that letter of the alphabet; criminal cases beginning *R*
v. — are at the beginning of the letter R. If the title of the case is
Re Smith, or *Ex p. Smith*, look under *Smith*. When you have traced
the case your require, you will find an entry similar to the
following:

Biles *v.* Caesar [1957] 1 W.L.R. 156; 101 S.J. 108; [1957] 1
All E.R. 151; [101 S.J. 141; 21 Conv. 169], C.A. . . . .
Digested, 57/1943: *Followed*, 59/1834: *Applied*, 68/2181;
69/2037.

At first this mass of information may look confusing. However,
it is well worth taking the trouble to find out what it means
because you are being provided with the complete "life history" of
a case: where and when it was originally reported, where you can
find periodical articles explaining the meaning of the case, and
perhaps criticising the decision, and in which cases the decision in
Biles v. *Caesar* has been quoted in court, and whether the court to
which it was quoted agreed with the decision of the judges in *Biles* v.
Caesar.

Let us look at each part of the entry in turn, to find out what it means.

(1) After the name of the case (*Biles* v. *Caesar*) you have a list of three places where you can find a full report of the case:

[1957] 1 W.L.R. 156, *i.e.* in the first of the three volumes of the *Weekly Law Reports* for 1957, at page 156.

101 S.J. 108 — in Volume 101 of the *Solicitors' Journal* at page 108 (this, as its name suggests, is a periodical, which you will find shelved with the periodicals).

[1957] 1 All E.R. 151 — in the first volume of the *All England Law Reports* for 1957, at page 151.

(2) The entries which are completely enclosed in square brackets — [101 S.J. 141; 21 Conv. 169] — are references to articles or comments in legal journals where the case is discussed in some detail. If you turn to Volume 101 of the *Solicitors' Journal*, or Volume 21 of the *Conveyancer*, you will find articles discussing the case of *Biles* v. *Caesar*.

(3) You will find that all the abbreviations which have been used — S.J., Conv., W.L.R., etc. — are listed at the front of the **Current Law Case Citator**, showing the full title of the journal or law report.

(4) The word *Digested* followed by the figures 57/1943 indicates that you will find a digest (a summary) of the case in the 1957 volume of the *Current Law Year Book*. Every item in the 1957 volume has its own individual number; you will find that item 1943 is a summary of the facts and decision in the case of *Biles* v. *Caesar*.

(5) You may sometimes wish to know whether the decision given in a particular case has been approved subsequently, *i.e.* when the case has been quoted in another court in support of an argument. The case of *Biles* v. *Caesar* has been quoted in court three times since it was originally decided — in 1959, when the decision was followed, and in 1968 and 1969 when the courts applied the decision of *Biles's* case to two other cases, following the doctrine of precedent. You can find the names of the cases in which *Biles* was referred to by looking in the 1959 *Current Law Year Book*, at item 1834, and in the 1968 and 1969 *Year Books*, at the item numbers given.

PROBLEMS

Using the **Current Law Case Citator** give the citation of:
Gibbings v. *Strong*
R. v. *Calvert*
Sheridan v. *Durkin*

If you are unable to find the case you require in the *Current Law Case Citator* or *Current Law Citator,* it is likely to be (a) an old case, or (b) a very recent case, *i.e.* within the last year, or (c) not an English case. If you think that it is likely to be a very recent case, follow the procedure outlined in para. 2-17.

2-15.   *Tracing a Case in the English and Empire Digest*

Older cases, and cases heard in Scottish, Irish and Commonwealth courts, can be traced by using the **English and Empire Digest**. This consists of the main work, four *Continuation Volumes*, and a *Cumulative Supplement*.

Turn to Volumes 52 to 54 of the **English and Empire Digest**. These are a *Consolidated Table of Cases* (*i.e.* a list of the names of cases, in alphabetical order). These volumes include English, Scottish, Irish and Commonwealth cases (including very old cases) but not any cases reported after 1966. Look up the name of the case you want in the alphabetical sequence. (If you have any difficulty finding the name of the case, read the Publisher's Announcement on pages vii-viii, at the beginning of Volume 52, which explains the alphabetical arrangement used). Let us suppose that you want to find out where the case of *Carlill* v. *Carbolic Smoke Ball Co.* was reported in the law reports. The entry gives you the following information:

Carlill *v.* Carbolic Smoke Ball Co. (1892): **22** *Evid.* 263; **25** *Gaming* 416, 418; **39** *Revenue* 313.

HOW TO TRACE A SPECIFIC CASE AND ITS SUBSEQUENT HISTORY IN THE ENGLISH AND EMPIRE DIGEST

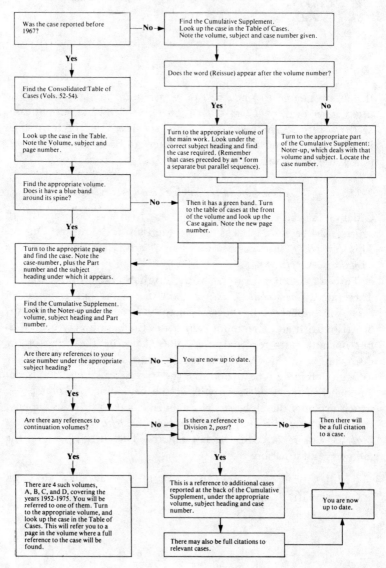

It is at this point that many students become confused. The reference given, *e.g.* 39 *Revenue* 313 is *not* an abbreviated version of the name of a volume of law reports which contains the report of the case. It is referring you to Volume 39 of the **English and Empire Digest**, where, at page 313, you will find (under the subject "Revenue") a summary of the case, and a list of all the places where the case has been reported. Finding a case is thus a two-stage process: (a) look up the case in Volumes 52 to 54; (b) look up the volume and page to which you are referred, and there you will find a list of places where the case has been reported.

You will notice that there are three entries in the index under *Carlill's* case. This means that the case deals with three different aspects of the law — the law of evidence, the law relating to gaming, and revenue law. You will find the same basic information (a list of citations to available reports of the case) under each of these three headings, but the summary of the case given will emphasise the aspects which are relevant to that heading. For instance, look up the second of the two references: 25 *Gaming* 416. If you turn to Volume 25 of the **English and Empire Digest** you will find that page 416 deals, as expected, with gaming laws. Under the heading "What is a contract by way of gaming and wagering" the second item, headed "Essentials of contract," is a summary of the relevant facts of *Carlill's* case. The name of the case is printed in capital letters at the end of the summary and this is followed by a list of citations to reports of the case in the *Law Reports* and various other series. In smaller type, under the heading "Annotations," there is a list of cases in which *Carlill's* case has subsequently been applied or referred to. (This covers cases up to 1961 (when the volume was compiled); if the case has been referred to in court since 1961, you can only trace this information by using the *Supplement* (see below)).

Let us suppose that we have decided to look up the first reference given: 22 *Evid.* 263. Here we encounter a problem. If you look at the spines of the volumes of the **English and Empire Digest**, you will notice that some of the numbers are on a blue background, whilst others are printed against a green background. The blue or green band across the back of each volume indicates the topicality of the information contained in that volume. The blue band volumes are being replaced by green band volumes, in which the information is more up to date. You will notice that the index volumes (including the *Consolidated Table of Cases*, in Volumes 52–54) have a blue band. This means that the information in the index volumes is correct if the volume you require has a blue band across the spine but if the volume you are referred to has a green band, the page numbers are likely to have changed from those given in the index. If we turn to Volume 22, which deals with Evidence, we notice that it has a green band across the spine. This means that it has been reissued and brought up to date since the information in the index volumes was published. The page number given in the *Consolidated Table of Cases* (page 263) is therefore likely to be inaccurate. Since we know the name of the case, we can look up the name of the case again in the *Table* (list) *of cases* which is printed at the front of Volume 22. As we suspected, when the volume was reissued the page number changed, and *Carlill's* case is now on page 295. On page 295, at item 2724, you will find a summary of those aspects of the case which are relevant to the law of evidence, a list of citations to reports of the case, and a list of subsequent cases in which the original decision has been affirmed.

Let us suppose that you have looked up the name of the case in the *Consolidated Table of Cases* and have found a reference similar to the following:

Cooke *v.* Ckoy Ltd., *Re* (Can.): **A** *Mast. & S.* 1129

This is a reference, not to the main work, but to a Canadian case (Can.) which will be found in *Continuation Volume A*, under the heading "Master and Servant," at page 1129. The cases in the *Continuation Volumes A* and *B* (which cover cases between 1952 and 1966) are included in the index of cases in Volumes 52 to 54.

If you think that your case is more recent than 1966, you should look in the **Cumulative Supplement**, which contains a list of the cases which appeared in *Continuation Volumes C* and *D* (these cover cases reported between 1967 and 1975) and the cases contained in the back half of the *Supplement* itself (covering cases from 1976 onwards). This table of cases in the *Supplement* will also refer you to any case reported since 1966 which has since been included in any of the reissued "green band" volumes of the main work.

You will have noticed, in looking at the **English and Empire Digest**, that every individual case has been given its own number; also, some cases are printed in smaller type than others, and these have a different series of reference numbers. The cases in smaller type are Irish, Scottish or Commonwealth cases and the smaller type and different reference numbers are to enable you to distinguish them from English cases (which are in larger type).

If you find the case you require in the *Cumulative Supplement*, the reference you are given is to the volume number, the subject heading, and the item number (*not* the page number). An asterisk (*) appears in front of some of the item numbers; this indicates that they are Irish, Scottish or Commonwealth cases, which are printed in smaller type. To find a case given in the *Supplement*, turn to the appropriate (revised) volume (or to the *Continuation Volumes* or to the entry in the *Supplement* itself) (see Summary below) and look under the subject heading given. When you have done this, you will see that every entry is individually numbered. Note whether there is an asterisk in front of the number; if so, look amongst the cases in smaller type for the number you require.

SUMMARY: TRACING A CASE IN THE CONSOLIDATED TABLE OF CASES

(1) Look up the name of the case in Volumes 52 to 54. Does the volume to which you are referred have a blue or a green band across the spine?

(2) *Blue band.* Look in the volume at the page given, and you will find a list of places where the case has been reported. (A list of the abbreviations used appears at the front of Volume 1 of the **English and Empire Digest**).

(3) *Green band.* Turn to the volume to which you have been referred. Look up the name of the case again, in the list of cases at the front of the volume, and find the page number given in that list. There you will find the details of the case.

(4) If the case does not appear in Volumes 52 to 54 look in the *Cumulative Supplement* (see below).

TRACING A CASE IN
THE CUMULATIVE SUPPLEMENT

(1) If the case is after 1966 look in the Table of Cases at the front of the *Cumulative Supplement.*

(2) The entry may be of two types:

    (a) If the word "Reissue" appears after the volume number, look in the appropriate green band volume of the main work, under the heading and case number given. (Cases preceded by an asterisk are in a separate but parallel numerical sequence, in smaller type.)

    (b) If the word "Reissue" does not appear after the volume number, turn to the second part of the *Cumulative Supplement* (*Division I — Noter Up*). Look up the entry in the *Noter Up* under the volume number, subject heading and case number given in the Table of Cases.

        You may find that the entry in the *Noter Up* refers you to a *Continuation Volume,* or to *Division 2, post.*

        If the reference is to a *Continuation Volume,* look up the name of the case in the index at the front of the relevant Continuation volume. This will refer you to the page containing your case.

        If you are referred to *Division 2, post,* turn to the back half of the *Cumulative Supplement* (*Additional Cases*) and look under the same volume, subject heading and case number that you consulted in the *Noter Up.*

PROBLEMS

Give the citation of:
Blake v. *Gibbs*
Small v. *Nairne*
Sobell v. *Boston*

2-16.   *Tracing a Case in Indexes to Law Reports*

In addition to the **Current Law Citators** and the **English and Empire Digest**, there are a number of indexes to the cases in individual series of law reports. For instance, the **All England**

Law Reports has published a volume containing a list of all the cases in the *All England Law Reports Reprint* (see para. 2-11), which covers selected cases between 1558 and 1935. In addition, there are three volumes containing the *Consolidated Tables and Index 1936–1976*. Volume 1 contains a list of all the cases included in the *All England Law Reports* between those dates. (The reference given is to the year, volume number and page number). More recent cases (since 1976) appear in the cumulative *Tables and the Index* and the *Current Cumulative Tables and Index* (see para. 2-17).

If you know that the case you are looking for is old, you can turn to the Index in Volumes 177 and 178 of the **English Reports**, and this will tell you if the case has been printed in the *English Reports* (see para. 2-10). Several other series of law reports also publish indexes and these can be useful if you know that a case is reported in a particular series but you have been given an incorrect reference.

The indexes to the **Law Reports** are very useful. From 1865 to 1949 a series of **Law Reports: Digests** were published. These contain summaries of the cases reported in the *Law Reports* in subject order, and a list of cases is usually included. From 1950 this has been published as the **Law Reports Consolidated Index** (lettered on the spine **Law Reports Index**). Two bound volumes have been published, covering 1951–1960 and 1961–1970 cases. An annual paper-covered "red" index is published, containing cases from 1971 to the end of the last year, and this is supplemented by a "pink" index, issued at intervals during the year, which lists all the cases published during the current year. The main arrangement of all the indexes is by subject, but there is an alphabetical list of *Cases Reported* at the front of each volume, and a list of *Cases Judicially Considered* at the back of the volumes. In addition to cases published in the *Law Reports*, the **Indexes** also include cases published in the *All England Law Reports*, *Criminal Appeal Reports*, *Lloyds Law Reports*, *Local Government Reports*, *Road Traffic Reports* and *Tax Cases*. If the *Current Law Citators* are not available in your library, this Index to the *Law Reports* will fulfill a similar function.

2-17.　　　HOW TO TRACE VERY RECENT CASES

If the case you want has been reported within the last year or so, you will not find it in the *Current Law Citators*, nor in the *English and Empire Digest*. If, therefore, you think that a case is likely to be very recent, you should adopt a different approach. Look in the latest issue of *Current Law*, at the list of cases printed at the front of each issue. If the name of your case appears, the reference given is to the monthly issue of *Current Law*, and to the individual item number within that issue, where you will find a summary of the case, and a note of where it has been reported. For example, suppose the case gives a reference such as: Jan 129. This means that if you look in the January issue of *Current Law*, item 129 (not page 129) is a summary of the case, with a list of places where the case is reported in full.

Other sources which can be used to trace a recent case are the indexes to the **Law Reports** and the **All England Law Reports**. The "pink index" to the *Law Reports* will cover cases reported in several of the major series of law reports; the front cover will indicate the exact period covered by the index. If the case is too recent to be included in here, look in the latest copy of the *Weekly Law Reports* which contains a list of all the cases which have been reported since the last "pink" index was published. Cases in the *All England Law Reports* are included in the Indexes to the **Law Reports**, but in addition, a separate index to the series is published. The **All England Law Reports Tables and Index** covers cases reported in the series since 1976. The dark blue covered main cumulative Tables are supplemented by a pale blue publication, entitled **Current Cumulative Tables and Index**, which is replaced regularly and which contains all the most recent cases.

A very recent case (*i.e.* within the last week or two) can only be traced by examining the summaries of cases which appear in *The Times*, and in the various weekly journals, such as the *New Law Journal* or the *Solicitors' Journal* (that is, assuming that you cannot trace it in the index in the latest copy of the *Weekly Law Reports*).

SUMMARY: TRACING WHERE A CASE HAS BEEN REPORTED

1. If the date is unknown, look in the *Current Law Case Citator* and *Current Law Citator* (see para. 2-14). If not traced

there, look in the *English and Empire Digest* (Vols. 52 to 54, and the *Cumulative Supplement*) (see para. 2-15).

2. If the case is thought to be old, look in the index to the *English Reports*, or the Index to the *All England Law Reports Reprint*; if not there, the *English and Empire Digest,* Vols. 52 to 54.

3. If the case is thought to be very recent look in latest issue of *Current Law* (see para. 2-17), or in the "pink" index to the *Law Reports* (see para. 2-16), and then in the latest issue of the *Weekly Law Reports* (see para. 2-17).

4. If the case is known to have been reported in one of the leading series but the reference you have is incorrect, look in the index to that series, if there is one, otherwise try *Current Law Citators* and the *English and Empire Digest*.

5. For a Scottish case, look in the separate list of Scottish cases at the back of the *Scottish Current Law Citators*; if not available, or not traced here, look in the *English and Empire Digest*.

6. For Irish cases check the *Irish Digest* or the *Index to Northern Ireland Cases*, (if available) or the *English and Empire Digest*.

7. For Commonwealth cases check the *English and Empire Digest*.

2-18.   HOW TO TRACE PERIODICAL ARTICLES AND
             COMMENTARIES ON A CASE

You may wish to discover if any periodical articles have been written about a case or to trace comments on a recent court decision. Such articles and comments usually explain the significance of the case and relate it to other decisions on the same aspect of the law. Sometimes writers who disagree with a decision may even argue that the case provides a justification for a change in the law.

Periodical articles on a case can be traced by using the **Current Law Citators** or the **Index to Legal Periodicals**. If you look again at the specimen entry (*Biles* v. *Caesar*) from the *Current Law Case Citator* (para 2-14) you will recall that the entries which were completely enclosed in square brackets were periodical articles on that case. Let us suppose that the case you are interested in is more recent, and is not included in the latest issue of the *Current Law Citators*. In this case you should look at the latest monthly issue of **Current Law**. In it you will find a **cumulative case citator**. If the name of your case appears here, is it printed in *italic* type? If so, this may mean that there has been a periodical article on the case during the current year (or the case has been judicially considered during the present year.) Turn to the monthly issue of *Current Law* indicated, and then to the item number. There you will either find another case in which your case has been cited, or a note of a periodical article on the case.

You can also trace articles on a case by looking in the back of the copies of the **Index to Legal Periodicals** (para. 4-4), under the heading "Table of Cases Commented Upon." Many of these will be American cases, but important English cases are included, if there has been a fairly lengthy article written about them.

If you know roughly when the case was decided, you can look in weekly journals, such as the *New Law Journal*, and in the various relevant specialist periodicals (such as the *Criminal Law Review*) published at that time, to see if there were any shorter editorial comments or criticisms of the decision. Publications such as *Law Notes* and the *Students' Law Reporter* will highlight the significance of the decision, and *The Law Teacher* may provide a more extended commentary on significant cases. The *Law Quarterly Review*, *Modern Law Review* and more specialist journals such as *Public Law*, the *Criminal Law Review*, and *The Conveyancer* usually include notes and comments on recent cases. Because these are relatively short they often do not appear in the list of periodical articles printed in *Current Law*. So, if you are looking for comments on recent cases, it is often easier to look through the pages and editorial columns of recent issues of the relevant specialist journals. Remember that general periodical articles may include a discussion of the case. Suppose, for instance, that you are interested in the 1978 case *Davis* v. *Johnson*, which is about a "battered mistress" who was successful in having the man who was ill-treating her evicted from the house in which they were living. Shortly after the case there were a number of periodical articles on domestic violence and the rights of cohabitees (these can be traced in *Current Law*, under the rather, in this case, misleading heading of "Husband and Wife"). Obviously many of these articles will discuss the case of *Davis* v.

Johnson, even though the name of the case is not actually mentioned in the title of the article.

PROBLEMS

Using the *Current Law Case Citator*, state the periodical articles concerned with *Overseas Tankship (U.K.)* v. *Morts Dock and Engineering Co. (The Wagon Mound)* [1961] A.C. 388.

Chapter 3

LEGISLATION

3-1.   INTRODUCTION

When a Bill (para. 5-6) has been approved by both Houses of
Parliament and has received the Royal Assent it normally becomes
law immediately. The first printed version of an Act to become
available is the Queen's Printer copy (published by HMSO), which
is issued within a few days of the Act receiving the Royal Assent.

A copy of an Act is reproduced opposite, which enables you to
become familiar with its various parts and with the way in which
Acts are cited.

3-2.   PARTS OF AN ACT

The different parts of an Act are:

1   Short title
2   Official citation
3   Long title
4   Date of Royal Assent
5   Enacting formula
6   Section and subsection
7   Marginal note
8   Date of commencement

If Schedules or Tables are included they are printed at the end of
the Act.

3-3.   CITATION OF STATUTES

Statutes (or Acts) are commonly referred to by a shortened version
of their title (the short title) and the year of publication, *e.g.* the
Theft Act 1968. Every Act published in a year is given its own
individual number and Acts may also be cited by the year in which
they were passed and the Act (or chapter) number. Thus the Theft
Act was the sixtieth Act passed in 1968 and is cited as 1968,

ELIZABETH II

Roe Deer (Close Seasons) Act 1977 ①

1977 CHAPTER 4 ②

An Act to Amend the Deer Act 1963 with respect to close seasons for roe deer. ③ [17th March 1977] ④

B E IT ENACTED by the Queen's most Excellent Majesty, by and with the advice and consent of the Lords Spiritual and Temporal, and Commons, in this present Parliament assembled, and by the authority of the same, as follows:— ⑤

1. Schedule 1 to the Deer Act 1963 (which prescribes close seasons for deer of the species and descriptions therein mentioned) shall be read and have effect as if under the heading " Roe Deer (Capreolus capreolus) " in the said Schedule there were inserted the words— *Close seasons for roe deer. 1963 c. 36.*

" Buck.......1st November to 31st March inclusive.". ⑥

2.—(1) This Act may be cited as the Roe Deer (Close Seasons) Act 1977. *Short title, and commencement.* ⑦

(2) This Act shall come into force on the 1st day of November 1977. ⑧

Illustration IV

chapter 60. "Chapter" is abbreviated to "c." when written, but it is spoken in full. (The use of this word dates from early days when all the legislation passed during one session of Parliament was referred to as a statute, *e.g.* the Statute of Merton, and each individual Act formed a separate chapter within the Statute.)

The present system of citing statutes by their year and chapter number began in 1963. Before that date the system was more complicated. Prior to 1963 statutes were referred to by the year of the monarch's reign (the "regnal year") and the chapter number. For example, a citation 3 Edw. 7, c.36 is a reference to the Motor Car Act 1903, which was the thirty sixth Act passed in the third year of the reign of Edward VII. A session of Parliament normally commences in the autumn and continues through into the summer of the following year. A "regnal year" is reckoned from the date of the sovereign's accession to the throne and a session of Parliament may therefore cover more than one regnal year. In the case of Queen Elizabeth II, who came to the throne in February, the first part of a Parliamentary session, from the autumn until February, falls into one regnal year, whilst the latter part of the session of Parliament falls into a different regnal year. Statutes passed before February bear a different regnal year to those passed after the anniversary of her accession to the throne. Two examples make this clearer:

The Children and Young Persons Act 1956 received the Royal Assent in March 1956, when the Queen had just entered the fifth year of her reign. It was the twenty-fourth Act to receive the Royal Assent during the Parliament which commenced sitting in the autumn of the fourth year of her reign, and which continued in session during the early part of the fifth year of her reign. The Act is therefore cited as 4 & 5 Eliz. 2, c.24.

By contrast, the Air Corporations Act 1956 was passed during the following session of Parliament and it received the Royal Assent in December 1956, when the Queen was still in the fifth year of her reign. Since, at that time, there could be no certainty that the Queen would still be on the throne in two months' time or that Parliament would still be in session in February, when she would be entering the sixth year of her reign, the statute was cited as 5 Eliz. 2, c.3 (*i.e.* the third Act passes in the Parliament held in the fifth year of the reign). When the Queen subsequently survived to enter her sixth year, the statute would henceforth be referred to as 5 & 6 Eliz. 2, c.3.

Both these Acts are to be found in the 1956 volumes of the statutes, which contain all the Acts passed during that year, regardless of the session of Parliament in which they were passed.

Until 1939, the volumes of the statutes contained all the Acts passed in a particular session of Parliament. After that date, the annual volumes contain all the statutes passed in a calendar year. This can give rise to some confusion. For instance, the volume for 1937 contains the statutes passed in the parliamentary session which extended from November 1936 to October 1937. Thus, some Acts which actually bear the date 1936 are included in the 1937 volume. The volume for 1938 includes some statutes passed between October and December of 1937 (which one might normally expect to find in the 1937 volume.)

3-4.   *Citation of the Names of Monarchs and their Regnal Years*

The names of the monarchs are abbreviated as follows:

Anne	Ann.
Charles	Car., Chas, *or* Cha.
Edward	Edw. *or* Ed.
Elizabeth	Eliz.
George	Geo.
Henry	Hen.
James	Ja., Jac. *or* Jas.
Mary	Mar. *or* M.
Philip and Mary	Ph. & M.
Richard	Ric. *or* Rich.
Victoria	Vict.
William	Will., Wm. *or* Gul.
William and Mary	W. & M., Wm. & M., Will. & Mar. *or* Gul. & Mar.

A list of the regnal years of monarchs showing the equivalent calendar year, will be found in *Sweet & Maxwell's Guide to Law*

Reports and Statutes (4th ed.), pp. 21–33; in J. E. Pemberton, *British Official Publications* (2nd ed.), pp. 120–125 and at the back of *Osborn's Concise Law Dictionary*.

3-5.   EDITIONS OF THE STATUTES

3-6.   *Modern Statutes — Official Editions*

Official copies of the Public General Acts are published individually by HMSO as soon as they receive the Royal Assent. The publication of a new Act is recorded in the *Daily List of Government Publications* (see para. 5-14).

3-7.   PUBLIC GENERAL ACTS AND MEASURES

At the end of the year, all Acts published during the year are bound together to form the official **Public General Acts and Measures of 19. . .** This series of red volumes has been published since 1831 (originally under the title *Public General Acts*). At the front of the annual volume will be found a list of all the Acts passed during the year, in alphabetical order, showing where they are to be found in the bound volume. There is also a chronological list (*i.e.* a list in chapter number order) giving the same information. The General Synod Measures of the Church of England are also printed in full in the annual volumes of the *Public General Acts*. A list of Local and Personal Acts (see para. 3-21) published during the year is printed in the annual volumes, but the texts of Local and Personal Acts are published separately.

3-8.   STATUTES IN FORCE

This is a new edition of the publication formerly known as *Statutes Revised*. It is especially useful for tracing legislation on a particular subject, and for that reason we shall look at it in more detail in para. 6-17.

3-9.   *Modern Statutes — Unofficial Collections*

3-10.   LAW REPORTS: STATUTES

The Incorporated Council of Law Reporting publishes, as part of the *Law Reports*, a series entitled **Law Reports: Statutes**. These are issued in several parts each year, each part containing the text of one or more Acts. At the end of the year the loose parts are replaced by an annual volume or volumes. Unfortunately, the loose parts are often not published until nearly a year after the Act receives the Royal Assent, so you must look elsewhere for the text of recent Acts (*e.g.* in the individual copies published by HMSO or in annotated versions of the statutes (para. 3-11)).

PROBLEMS

(a) Give the title of the Act which is referred to as 1975, c. 77.

(b) Give the official citation of the Town and Country Planning Act 1971.

(c) To what Act does the citation 5 & 6 Eliz., c. 27 refer?

(d) The Representation of the People Act 1949 was passed in a parliamentary session which spanned three regnal years. What is the citation which appears at the top of the Act?

How does this differ from the citation which appears on the spine of the bound volume which contains the statutes passed in 1949?

(e) Locate the Public Order Act, 1 Edw. 3 & 1 Geo. 6, c. 6. What was the date of this Act?

What year is printed on the outside of the volume in which this Act is to be found?

What is the reason for this discrepancy?

3-11. ANNOTATED EDITIONS OF THE STATUTES

If your library does not receive all the statutes automatically, as soon as they receive the Royal Assent, then the first copy of a new Act which appears in the library is likely to be an annotated version (*i.e.* the text of the Act is printed and notes are also included on the meaning of words and phrases used in the Act, the effect of the Act, etc.). Such annotated versions of the statutes can be very helpful but you should be aware that the notes have no official standing. Three annotated versions of the statutes are generally available: *Current Law Statutes Annotated, Halsbury's Statutes* and *Butterworth's Annotated Legislation Service*.

3-12. *Current Law Statutes Annotated*

Current Law Statutes Annotated are issued in a number of parts each year, each part usually covering several Acts. They are published several months after the Acts included received the Royal Assent. The notes explain the meaning of words and phrases used and state the provisions of each section of the Act in relatively simple language, showing the relationship of the new law to existing legislation and case law. The notes are printed in smaller type so that the commentary can be readily distinguished from the actual text of the Act. At the end of the year the loose parts are replaced by an annual volume. If your library subscribes to the Scottish edition of *Current Law*, this annual volume may be entitled **Scottish Current Law Statutes**. Despite the title, this contains all the legislation relating to England, as well as Scotland. *Current Law Statutes* have been published since 1948.

3-13. *Butterworth's Annotated Legislation Service*

Butterworth's Annotated Legislation Service was formerly called *Butterworth's Emergency Legislation Service*. It reprints the text of selected Acts, with notes. Many of the volumes cover only one Act, with very detailed annotations. From time to time a cumulative index to the series is published, which lists all the Acts passed since 1939 and shows where they are to be found in the series. A number of the titles in this series have also been published individually as books, *e.g.* R. M. Goode, *Introduction to the Consumer Credit Act 1974*. The emphasis is on statutes which will be of use to the practitioner. For those statutes which are covered in the series the service provides the best annotated version of the Act which is available.

3-14. *Halsbury's Statutes of England*

This is particularly useful for tracing Acts on a particular subject. For that reason it is more fully described elsewhere (para. 6-19). If you know the name or date of an Act you can look this information up in the alphabetical and chronological lists which appear at the front of the Index to Volumes 1—45. These will tell you the volume and page number in **Halsbury's Statutes** where you will find the text of the Act reprinted, with annotations. If you are looking for an Act passed after 1975, look in the alphabetical and chronological list at the front of the *Cumulative Supplement* to locate the relevant volume. You should, however, note that Acts dealing with more than one subject may be split up so that only part of a particular Act may be printed under a subject heading. The annotated text of Acts passed during the current year can be found in the looseleaf *Current Statutes Service* volume at the end of the bound volumes.

3-15. *Older Statutes*

So far we have been concerned with modern statutes. However, it will sometimes be necessary to examine an Act of Parliament which dates back several centuries. The earliest statute which is still part of the law of the land was passed in 1267. The first parliamentary statutes date from 1235 (the Statute of Merton) although some collections of the statutes commence in 1225. Collections of the legislation prior to 1225 do exist (*e.g.* A. J. Robertson, *The Laws of the Kings of England from Edmund to Henry I*) but they are not regarded as forming part of the Statutes of the Realm.

3-16. *Collections of Older Statutes*

3-17. STATUTES OF THE REALM

Produced by the Record Commission, **Statutes of the Realm** is generally regarded as the most authoritative collection of the early statutes. It covers statutes from 1235 to 1713, including those no longer in force, and prints the text of all Private Acts before 1539. There are alphabetical and chronological indexes of all the Acts and there is a subject index to each volume, as well as an index to the complete work.

3-18.　STATUTES AT LARGE

The title of **Statutes at Large** was given to various editions of the statutes, most of which were published during the eighteenth century. They normally cover statutes published between the thirteen and the eighteenth or nineteenth centuries.

3-19.　ACTS AND ORDINANCES OF THE INTERREGNUM

Acts passed during the Commonwealth are excluded from the collections of the statutes mentioned above. They can be found in C. H. Firth and R. S. Rait, *Acts and Ordinances of the Interregnum, 1642–1660*.

3-20.　STATUTES REVISED

A complete collection of all statutes, of whatever date, in force in December 1948 was published in the **Statutes Revised** (3rd ed.). A new edition (called **Statutes in Force**) is at present being published (para. 6-17). Older statutes which are still part of the law of the land are reprinted in **Halsbury's Statutes** (para. 6-19).

The various indexes to the statutes, which enable you to trace all the legislation on a particular subject which is still in force, are dealt with in Chapter 6.

SUMMARY OF THE COLLECTIONS
OF STATUTES

TEXT OF OLDER STATUTES
Statutes of the Realm (1235–1713)
Statutes at Large (1225 — approx. 1869) (depending on the editions available in your library)
MODERN STATUTES
Public General Acts and Measures (1831 — date)
Law Reports: Statutes (1866 — date)

ANNOTATED VERSIONS
Current Law Statutes (1948 — date)
Halsbury's Statutes of England
Butterworth's Annotated Legislation Service (1939 — date)
COLLECTIONS OF STATUTES IN FORCE
Halsbury's Statutes of England
Statutes Revised (a collection of statutes in force in 1948)
Statutes in Force (still being published)

3-21.   LOCAL AND PERSONAL ACTS

In addition to Public General Acts, which apply to the whole population, or a substantial part of it, there are also published each year a few Local and Personal Acts. These Acts affect only a particular area of the country or a particular individual or body, *e.g.* Plymouth City Council Act 1975; James Hugh Maxwell (Naturalisation) Act 1975; Brookwood Cemetery Act 1975.

3-22.   *Citation of Local and Personal Acts*

In the case of a Local Act, the chapter number is printed in roman numerals, to distinguish it from the Public General Act of the same number. Thus the Brookwood Cemetery Act may be cited as 1975, c. xxxv (*i.e.* the 35th Local Act passed in 1975), whilst 1975, c. 35 is the citation for a Public Act, the Farriers (Registration) Act.

Personal Acts are cited in the same way as Public General Acts, but with the chapter number printed in italics, *e.g.* c.*3*. The citation of Local and Personal Acts was amended in 1963. Prior to that date they are cited by regnal years, in the same way as Public General Acts; *e.g.* 12 & 13 Geo. 5, c.xiv relates to a local Act, whilst 12 & 13 Geo. 5, c.14 is a Public Act (para. 3-3).

Bills may be introduced into Parliament by a private Member of Parliament, as well as by Ministers. When this happens the Bill, if approved by Parliament, becomes a Public General Act. Private Members Bills do not, therefore, automatically become Private Acts. (It is worth noting that Private Members' Bills are not normally published by HMSO, but are published and distributed by the Members themselves.)

Although most libraries will possess copies of the Public General Acts in some form, the Local and Personal Acts are not so widely available, as they are not printed in the volumes of *Public General Acts*, nor in any of the other major collections of statutes.

3-23.   *Indexes to Local and Personal Acts*

Indexes to Local and Personal Acts are: the **Index to Local and Personal Acts** 1801–1947; the **Supplementary Index to the Local and Personal Acts** 1948–1966, and the **Local and Personal Acts 19 : Tables and Index** (published annually). A list (but not the text) of Local and Personal Acts passed during the year is included in the annual volumes of *Public General Acts*. More recent Acts can be traced in the daily and monthly lists of government publications (see para. 5-14).

3-24.   DELEGATED LEGISLATION

In an attempt to reduce the length and complexity of statutes, Parliament may grant to some other authority (usually a Minister of the Crown) power to make detailed rules and regulations on a topic which has been covered in more general terms by an Act of Parliament. For instance, the various Road Traffic Acts give the Secretary of State for Transport power, amongst other things, to impose speed limits on particular stretches of road, to vary these limits at any time, to create experimental traffic schemes, introduce new road signs, control the construction and use of vehicles, and impose regulations concerning parking, pedestrian crossings, vehicle licences, insurance and numerous other aspects of the law relating to motor vehicles. An advantage of this power is that the rules can be readily changed, without the necessity for Parliamentary approval of every case. One disadvantage is that all the regulations (over 2,000 of them are issued every year) are part of the law of the land, and the citizen may be expected to be acquainted with each and every one of them — a task which is clearly impossible.

3-25.   *The Nature of Statutory Instruments*

Delegated (or subordinate) legislation is a phrase which covers a number of different terms. Regulations, rules, orders and by-laws are terms which describe delegated legislation but, whatever the term used, they are all statutory instruments. Whenever Parliament has conferred the power to make delegated legislation the document by which this power is exercised is called a statutory instrument. Like statutes, statutory instruments may be of general or of purely local interest; local instruments (*e.g.* by-laws) are not always printed and published in the normal way. An Order in Council, made by the Queen and her Privy Council, is also a form of statutory instrument, and these are printed as an appendix to the annual volumes of statutory instruments, together with Royal Proclamations and Letters Patent.

3-26.   *Citation of Statutory Instruments*

Several statutory instruments are published by HMSO on most working days. Every instrument published during the year is given its own individual number. The official citation is: S.I. year/number. For example, The Criminal Law Act 1977 (Commencement No. 2) Order 1977 was the one thousand four hundred and twenty-sixth statutory instrument to be passed in 1977 and its citation is therefore S.I. 1977/1426.

3-27.   *Tracing Statutory Instruments*

The statutory instruments published each day are listed in the **Daily List of Government Publications**. Every week a summary of the most important new instruments is printed in the coloured pages of the *New Law Journal*. The *Solicitors' Journal*, many specialist journals, and *Current Law*, all note recent changes in the law which have been brought about by statutory instruments. A **List of Statutory Instruments** is published monthly, showing the instruments published during a particular month; these monthly issues are replaced by an annual list.

In addition to containing a list of all the instruments issued during the period, in numerical order, the *List of Statutory Instruments* also prints the instruments under subject headings; a detailed Subject Index is provided, so that changes in the law relating to a particular topic can be easily traced.

The individual statutory instruments (which may not be

available in all libraries) are replaced by a number of bound volumes which cover the instruments published during a particular year. The instruments are now printed in these volumes in numerical order, although, until 1961, they were arranged by subject. The last volume of each yearly set of volumes now contains a subject index to all the instruments published during that year.

Statutory instruments on a subject can be traced by using the **Index to Government Orders** (see para. 6-28) together with the annual and monthly *Lists of Statutory Instruments*, which bring the information up to date. **Halsbury's Statutory Instruments** (see para. 6-27) can also be used to trace statutory instruments dealing with a particular subject.

All the statutory instruments which were still in force at the end of 1948 were reprinted in a series of volumes entitled **Statutory Rules and Orders and Statutory Instruments Revised**. This was arranged in subject order, showing all the instruments which were then in force. It is possible to check whether a particular instrument is still in force by using the **Table of Government Orders** (see para. 6-31) or by checking in *Halsbury's Statutory Instruments* (see para. 6-27).

If your library does not possess a complete set of statutory instruments (and many of the volumes are no longer available) then you may be able to trace the text of the instrument in *Halsbury's Statutory Instruments* or in one of the many specialist looseleaf encyclopedias which are now being published *e.g.* the *Encyclopedia of Housing Law and Practice*. Failing this, a summary may often be found in *Current Law* or the *Current Law Year Book* under the appropriate subject heading (there is a list at the beginning of each Year Book showing where each instrument appears in the volume.)

PROBLEMS

(a) Name the statutory instrument for which the official citation is: S.I. 1977/1212.

(b) Consult the subject index in the last bound volume of statutory instruments published in 1976 (Part III, Section 3) and give the name of the statutory instrument on hi-jacking which relates to the protection of aircraft. What is the number of the statutory instrument?

(c) At the end of every statutory instrument there appears a Note. What does this contain? Is this Note part of the statutory instrument (*i.e.* does it have the force of law)?

Chapter 4

PERIODICALS

4-1.   TYPES OF PERIODICALS

Periodicals are important as they are designed to keep you up to date with the latest developments in common and statute law and also to provide informed comment and criticism of the law. Thus, they aid you in the transitional process of being more than simply a competent legal technician and direct you towards fulfilling the wider aims of academic legal education. In your seminar, essay and moot preparations an appreciation of the available periodical literature is essential, for you cannot rely exclusively on textbooks which are always, to some degree, out of date and which may provide inadequate information on some topics. You should develop the habit of glancing at the title pages of recently published periodicals, which are normally kept on a separate display shelf. This will help to keep you up to date with recent cases, statutes, official publications, comments and scholarly articles.

For convenience, we can divide periodicals into four different groups, although there is some overlap between them. They are treated similarly in libraries. There are a number of weekly publications, such as the *New Law Journal, Justice of the Peace, Solicitors' Journal* and *Law Society Gazette*, which aim to keep practitioners and students up to date. They provide reports and comments on recent cases, statutes, statutory instruments, and the latest trends and developments in the law, together with some longer articles, usually on topical or practical subjects. In contrast are the academic journals, published less frequently, which contain lengthy articles on a variety of topics, comments on recent cases, statutes and government publications, and book reviews. Some examples are the *Cambridge Law Journal* (twice a year), *Law Quarterly Review, Modern Law Review* (six a year) and the *British Journal of Law and Society* (twice a year). The third category is the specialist journal dealing with particular aspects of the law. This type of journal combines notes of recent developments with longer articles on aspects of that area of the law. Examples of such specialist journals are the *Criminal Law Review* (monthly), *Industrial Law Journal* (four a year), *Legal Action Group Bulletin* (monthly) and the *Estates Gazette* (weekly). The final group is foreign periodicals. English language publications, particularly from common law jurisdictions, are of assistance in providing a comparative view of similar United Kingdom issues. Examples of this group are the *Yale Law Journal* (eight a year), *Harvard Law Review* (eight a year), *Canadian Bar Review* (four a year) and the *Australian Law Journal* (monthly).

4-2.   TRACING RELEVANT LEGAL PERIODICAL ARTICLES

When you are collecting relevant material you will be faced by two problems:

(1)   How can I discover what has been written on a given subject, or if any commentary has been published on a particular case, statute, Law Commission report, or other document?

(2)   Having found the details of apparently relevant material, how do I obtain a copy of the journal?

The answer to the first question lies in the proper use of various indexes to periodicals (including abstracts) and to answer the second query you must consult the periodicals catalogue or, possibly, a union list of periodicals.

We list a number of sources which can be used to trace periodical articles. You may not need, or wish, to consult all of them, but you should remember that the information given, and the journals covered, varies, and by using only one index you may miss helpful material.

4-3.   *Current Law*

Current Law commenced in 1947 and is arranged by subject (see paras. 6-9 and 6-10). At the end of each subject heading, in each of the monthly issues, is a list of recent periodical articles which have been published on that subject, including some shorter notes and comments on recent legislation and reports. There is also an

HOW TO TRACE LEGAL PERIODICAL ARTICLES

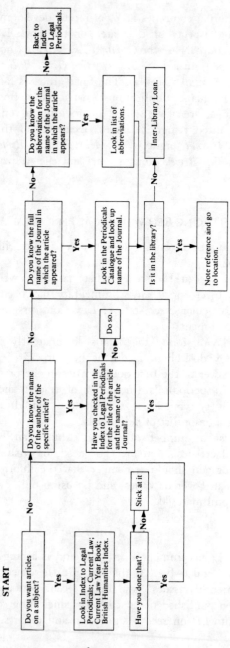

entry "articles" under subject headings in the cumulative index which is published in each issue, but this is not comprehensive, and you are advised to look through each of the monthly issues for the year, at the end of the appropriate subject, to ensure that nothing has been overlooked. When the **Current Law Year Book** is published, the index of periodical articles is found at the back of the volume. Since 1955, the list of periodical articles has been omitted from the end of each subject in the main part of the work. The preface to the **Current Law Year Book** gives further information regarding its use, as does the inside cover of Current Law. You should also familiarise yourself with the explanatory pamphlet *How to Use Current Law*.

PROBLEMS

(a)   Who wrote an article on income tax and the tax relief on books and periodicals in 1977?

(b)   In 1975, where was an article published on law enforcements in Northern Ireland?

4-4.   *Index to Legal Periodicals*

The **Index to Legal Periodicals** is an American publication which also includes journals from Britain, Canada, Ireland, Australia and New Zealand. However, you may need to use it in conjunction with the **Index to Foreign Legal Periodicals** (see para. 4-5). Some English language journals are included in the *Index to Foreign Legal Periodicals*. If in doubt about the journals covered consult the list of periodicals indexed. This list appears in each issue.

Entries are arranged under author and also under the subject, in one single alphabetical sequence. There is a separate index at the back of each issue which gives the names of cases which have been commented upon in periodical articles. The headings use American terminology and spelling and this may cause occasional difficulties but on the whole it is often easier to find entries on a relevant subject here than in *Current Law*. A typical subject entry is printed below, with numbered explanations:

CONTRACTS[1]: consideration
Bankers' commercial credits among the High Trees.[2] M. Clarke.[3] Camb. L.J. 33:260–92 N '74[4]
Contract restitution and total failure of consideration.[2] C.P. Seepersad.[3] New L.J. 123:435–8 My 10 '73.[5]

[1] subject heading
[2] title of article
[3] author
[4] in Cambridge Law Journal, Vol. 33, pp. 260–292 (dated November, 1974)
[5] article in New Law Journal, Vol. 123, pp. 435–438 (dated May 10, 1973)

A typical author entry is printed below:

SEEPERSAD, C.P.[1]
Contracts: consideration[2] (C)[3]
Restitution[2] (C)[3]

[1] author entry for the second of the specimen subject entries (above)
[2] headings under which articles by Seepersad appear
[3] first letter of the first word of the title (*i.e.* Contract. . .) of the article. The same article may appear under several subject headings. In this example it occurs under two headings.

A list of the subject headings used in the **Index**, and of all the abbreviations used, is found at the beginning of the volume. The **Index** is published several times a year and these copies are later replaced by an annual volume containing all the periodical articles for that year. The annual volumes are replaced by volumes (called "cumulations") covering articles written during a three year period. The **Index** commenced in 1908.

PROBLEMS

(a) If you wished to find periodical articles written about (i) "Doctors," (ii) "Conservation," what subject headings would you look under?

(b) Give the title, year, volume number, full name of the journal and page numbers for the article written by Jack A. Hiller between 1973 and 1976?

(c) Who wrote the article "Lawyers in an Open Society" (1972)? Look under "Legal Profession."

4-5.   *Index to Foreign Legal Periodicals*

The **Index to Foreign Legal Periodicals** commenced in 1960. It indexes articles on international and comparative law and the municipal law of all countries except the United States, United Kingdom and the common law of Commonwealth countries. Many of the articles are not in English. The series contains subject, geographical, book reviews and author indexes. Publication is usually on a three-year cycle, at the end of which a cumulative volume is produced.

PROBLEMS

(a) In which countries are the following journals published? (Consult the list of periodicals indexed):
Journal of African Law
Columbia Journal of Transnational Law
Scandinavian Studies in Law

(b) What does the abbreviation R43 represent in the list of periodicals indexed?

4-6.   *Halsbury's Laws*

Periodical articles written on a subject during a particular year may also be traced in the **Annual Abridgement to Halsbury's Laws** (see para. 6-5). At the beginning of the entry for each subject there is a list of periodical articles written on that subject during the year.

PROBLEM

Who wrote an article in 1974 on trade secrets? (Look under the heading "Employment.")

Finally, we introduce you to a short cut for establishing the literature in the field. First, find a recent article or text book on the subject you are investigating, then examine the footnotes. If well researched it will give you numerous citations to read. However, be warned, you may end up with an incomplete coverage and also possibly one which supports the view of the author!

4-7.   HOW TO TRACE LAW-RELATED PERIODICAL ARTICLES

The effective study of law will of necessity take you into other disciplines. Articles on subjects such as housing, delinquency, sentencing, families, and town and country planning are found in a range of journals, many of which are not solely concerned with law and which as a consequence are not usually found in a law collection. You may wish to consult journals in other sections of the general library which carry articles by sociologists, economists, criminologists, social administrators or historians. To trace social science and arts material on law-related topics will require recourse to a different selection of indexes, most of which will be housed outside the law collection.

4-8.   *Index to Periodical Articles Related to Law*

This index commenced in 1958. It contains a selective coverage of articles published in English throughout the world and which are not included in either the *Index to Legal Periodicals* or the *Index to Foreign Legal Periodicals*. It contains an index to articles by subject, a list of journals indexed and an author index. The first cumulative volume covered the period 1958–1968 and the second cumulative volume takes us up to and includes 1973. Thereafter, it appears quarterly, the last issue of a year being a cumulative issue.

PROBLEM

Name the article written on Legal Aid in Australia in June 1970 by J. J. Spigelman.

4-9. *The British Humanities Index*

This covers a wide range of subjects and includes articles in newspapers and popular weekly journals, as well as more scholarly periodicals. Entries are under subjects and authors.

4-10. *Social Sciences Index*

This Index, which replaces the *Social Sciences and Humanities Index*, covers law, criminology, sociology, political science, sociological aspects of medicine and other socio-legal topics. Entries are under authors and subjects.

4-11. *Abstracts on Criminology and Penology*

This is arranged by subject, each entry having its own individual number. There are detailed subject and author indexes referring to individually numbered entries.

4-12. *Psychological Abstracts*

The scope of this is far wider than the title suggests, covering abortion, drug use, alcoholics, etc. Entries are under subject and there are detailed subject and author indexes.

4-13.   *Current Contents: Social and Behavioural Sciences*

This covers the contents of recent issues of more than 1,300 journals in the social and behavioural sciences (including law). The arrangement is by subject, with author and "key word" subject indexes.

4-14.   *The Philosopher's Index*

It is a subject and author index with abstracts. Philosophy and inter-disciplinary publications are indexed.

4-15.   *Sociological Abstracts*

This abstracting service is indexed by subject and author. It includes sections on sociology of law, penology and correctional problems.

These are by no means the only subject indexes to the contents of periodicals. Indexes exist covering many different subjects. The library staff will help you find out which indexing or abstracting services are available to cover the subjects which interest you.

4-16.   NEWSPAPER ARTICLES

In addition to factual reporting, newspapers often contain commentary, analysis and background information on recent legal developments and controversial topics. Some libraries operate a cutting service of the "quality" newspapers such as *The Times* and *The Guardian*, as well as cutting out the law reports. Many libraries keep back copies of *The Times* or have them on microfilm. An **Index to The Times** which includes *The Sunday Times* is published which will help you identify and locate relevant material. Another source is **Keesing's Contemporary Archives**, established in 1931, which allows you to trace the date of a specific event. Thereafter you can turn to the newspapers and commentaries of that period.

4-17.   LOCATING PERIODICALS IN THE LIBRARY

Having traced an article how do you locate the relevant copy of the journal? The first problem may be to decipher the abbreviations which have been used for the name of the journal. If you obtained your information from a periodical index or from the **Current Law Citators** a list of the abbreviations will be found at the front of the volume. If the information was obtained from elsewhere, *e.g.* from a footnote in a textbook, look up the abbreviation in the **Index to Legal Periodicals** or associated indexes, in Sweet & Maxwell's **Guide to Law Reports and Statutes** or in **Where to Look for Your Law**.

Once the full title of the periodical is known, look up the name of the journal in the periodicals catalogue. The catalogue entry will guide you to the part of the library in which the journal is to be found, and will indicate which volumes of the journal are available in your library. If it is a law periodical they are usually arranged in alphabetical order. In a few cases the arrangement is less obvious (see para. 1-9).

4-18.   LOCATING PERIODICALS FROM OTHER SOURCES

If the journal is not available in your library you may wish to try to obtain it from elsewhere. Legal periodicals can be traced by consulting the **Union List of Legal Periodicals** (published by the University of London Institute of Advanced Legal Studies) which gives the location of journals in libraries throughout the country. Similar union lists are published covering more specialised subjects, such as air law literature, West European legal literature, Commonwealth and South African law, and United States legal literature. If you wish to consult a large number of journals or reports it may be more convenient to go to another library and use the material there. (Before doing so you should contact the librarian and ask for permission). If only a few articles are required it may be easier to ask your library to obtain them through the **interlibrary loan service**. Details of this service (which is normally free of charge to the individual) may be obtained from the interlibrary loans staff in your library. This national facility may be available to students as well as staff and is invaluable for materials not available in local law libraries. The library staff may also be able to advise on which periodicals are available in other libraries in the area.

Chapter 5

GOVERNMENT PUBLICATIONS

5-1. INTRODUCTION

Government publications, that is, mainly publications issued by Her Majesty's Stationery Office (HMSO) are notoriously difficult to use. In this chapter we shall look at the different types of government publications which are the most likely to be encountered by law students, *e.g.*

Command papers
House of Commons and House of Lords papers
Bills
Official reports of Parliamentary Debates (Hansard).

Further details of all the publications mentioned, together with specimen pages, may be found in an excellent book by John E. Pemberton, *British Official Publications*. A shorter guide is J. G. Ollé, *An Introduction to British Government Publications*. Acts of Parliament, which are, of course, government publications, have already been dealt with in Chapter 3.

This is a field in which you should not hesitate to seek the advice of library staff whenever you are in difficulty. Most libraries which have a collection of government publications have at least one person who is responsible for helping readers to use this material.

5-2. PARLIAMENTARY AND NON-PARLIAMENTARY PUBLICATIONS

HMSO publishes several thousand items each year. They divide their publications into two groups: parliamentary publications and non-parliamentary publications. It is often difficult to ascertain into which of these two categories an item falls but the distinction is important for in many libraries the two categories are treated differently.

Parliamentary publications (or **parliamentary papers**) are those documents which are required by Parliament in the course of its work, *e.g.* Bills, records of the proceedings in the House, and information Papers on a wide variety of topics. If your library has a complete collection of all parliamentary publications, these may be bound together in volumes containing all the material produced during a particular session of Parliament. These volumes are known as **sessional papers** or **sessional sets.** The conventional arrangement of the sessional papers divides the parliamentary papers relating to the House of Commons into four main groups, *i.e.*

Group	Comprising	
1. Bills	House of Commons Bills	Drafts of public Bills arranged in alphabetical order by the titles of the Bills.
2. Reports from Committees	House of Commons Papers	Reports from House of Commons committees.
3. Reports from Commissioners	House of Commons Papers and Command Papers	Reports from other committees, Royal Commissions, etc.
4. Accounts and papers	House of Commons Papers and Command Papers	Accounts, "white papers," estimates, Treaty series, and other state papers.

(The meaning of these various terms is fully explained later in this Chapter and in Appendix II).

The library usually does not enter these parliamentary publications in the library catalogues. Instead it relies on the indexes produced by Her Majesty's Stationery Office (para. 5-14) to trace relevant material in the collection.

More recent parliamentary publications (*i.e.* those published within the last two to three years) will usually be gathered together in boxes. Every Parliamentary paper has its own individual number and the papers will usually be arranged by these numbers in boxes comprising:

House of Commons Papers
House of Commons Bills
House of Lords Papers and Bills
Command Papers

These recent publications can also be traced through the various indexes to government publications (para. 5-14). You will probably find that all the parliamentary publications have been housed in an Official Publications collection, in a separate area of the library (which may not form part of the law library).

Non-parliamentary publications may be scattered throughout the library, according to the subjects with which they deal. Unlike parliamentary publications, they are normally entered in the library catalogues, usually under the heading "GREAT BRITAIN," followed by the name of the government department which produced the publication, *e.g.* GREAT BRITAIN. *Home Office*.

5-3.   PARLIAMENTARY PUBLICATIONS

We shall now look in more detail at some of the most important categories of parliamentary publications and how they are arranged in the library.

5-4.   *Command Papers*

This is a very important category of parliamentary papers and one to which you may frequently be referred. It includes many major government reports, *e.g. The Butler report on mentally abnormal offenders, The Renton report on the preparation of legislation*, some (but not all) of the reports of the Law Commission, and the reports of all Royal Commissions. A **Command Paper** is, as it states on the front cover, presented to Parliament "By Command of Her Majesty." In practice, this means that it is presented to Parliament by a Minister of the Crown on his own initiative; its preparation has not been requested by Parliament. **Command Papers** are often statements of government policy, and are likely to be the subject of future legislation, or they are presented for the information of Members of Parliament. **Command Papers** include:

statements of government policy (often referred to as "White Papers");

some annual statistics and annual reports (many more are issued as non-Parliamentary publications);

reports of Royal Commissions;

reports of some committees (other committee reports may be issued as non-Parliamentary publications);

reports of tribunals of enquiry, *e.g.* Report of the tribunal appointed to inquire into the Vassall Case. (Cmnd. 2009); state papers (including the Treaty series (para. 8-4)).

5-5.   CITATION AND LOCATION OF COMMAND PAPERS

Command Papers are each given an individual number, prefaced by an abbreviation for the word "command." This abbreviation, and the number, are printed at the bottom left hand corner of the cover of the report. The numbers used run on continuously from one session of Parliament to another. The present abbreviation, "Cmnd." has been used for publications issued since 1956. Prior to 1956 different abbreviations of the word "command" were used. They were:

1st series 1833-1869	[1] — [4222] (the abbreviation for "Command" was omitted in the first series)
2nd series 1870-1899	[C. 1] — [C. 9550]
3rd series 1900-1918	[Cd. 1] — [Cd. 9239]
4th series 1919-1956	[Cmd. 1] — Cmd. 9889
5th series 1956-date	Cmnd. 1 —

(The use of square brackets was abandoned in 1922). It is important to note exactly the form of the abbreviation so that you have some idea of the date of the report. For instance Cmd. 6404 which relates to social insurance and allied services (the Beveridge Report) is a completely different item from Cmnd. 6404, which is an international agreement relating to pensions. One was published in 1942 and the other in 1976.

If your library keeps all the **Command Papers** together in boxes, arranged by command numbers, you will have no difficulty in tracing the report you want. However if the publications are arranged by sessions or are bound into sessional sets, (see para. 5-2), it will be necessary to have some idea of the date of the **Command Paper**. You will find the *Concordance of Command Papers 1833–1972*, which is printed in *Pemberton*, pp. 65–66, of help. Occasionally, a report is published later than the **Command Papers** with adjoining numbers, with the result that it appears in a different session of Parliament (and is therefore in a different sessional set). If you know the command number, and wish to locate it in the bound sessional sets, first ascertain the correct session, by consulting *Pemberton's* list or the annual catalogues of **government publications** (see para. 5-14). Then go to the sessional index, which is in the last volume for each session. There you will find a list of command numbers indicating, for each one, the volume and page within the sessional set where it can be found.

State papers are bound together at the end of the sessional set (in the volumes labelled "Accounts" and "Papers"). One of the major categories of state papers is the **Treaty Series**. These are **Command Papers**, and each has a command number, but, in addition, each has its own Treaty Series number. If they are not bound into the sessional sets, the library may keep all the Treaty Series together. There are separate annual and three or four-yearly consolidated indexes to the series; in addition, they also appear in HMSO's catalogues of Government Publications. Both the Treaty Series number and the **Command Paper** numbers are given. In 1970, HMSO published an **Index of British Treaties 1101–1968** (compiled by Clive Parry and Charity Hopkins), (see para. 8-5). There are entries under subjects (Vol. 1) and by the date of the treaties (Vols. 2 and 3).

An explanation of how to trace a **Command Paper** on a particular subject (or how to trace a report if you know the name of the chairman) will be found later in this Chapter (paras. 5-20, 5-22).

5-6.   *Bills*

Bills (House of Lords and House of Commons) are draft versions of Acts of Parliament, which are laid before Parliament for their consideration and approval. If your library has a complete collection of parliamentary papers, the **Bills** will be shelved with this collection; if not, they may be available in the law library. If the library's parliamentary papers are bound up into sessional sets, the **Bills** will form the first volumes of each set. More recent **Bills** (*i.e.* those for the last two to three years) are likely to be shelved separately in boxes.

5-7. STAGES IN THE PASSAGE OF A BILL

Before a **Bill** can become law, it passes through a number of stages. These are:

(i) *first reading* – a purely formal reading of the **Bill's** title by the Clerk of the House; after this the **Bill** is printed and placed on sale to the public.

(ii) *second reading* – the principles of the **Bill** are discussed. If the **Bill** fails to gain the approval of the House at this stage it must be dropped. The debate is reported in **Hansard**; (see para. 5-11).

(iii) *Committee stage* – the whole House may sit as a committee to examine the **Bill**. More usually, the details of the **Bill** are referred to a standing committee for discussion. The **Parliamentary Debates: House of Commons: Official Reports of Standing Committees** debates are published separately from *Hansard*. They are issued daily, and each issue covers the discussions on one **Bill**. The daily copies are later replaced by bound volumes. There are various standing committees, and, when using the unbound copies it is necessary to find out which committee discussed the particular **Bill** you are interested in. This may be done by looking in the **Government Publications** Catalogue (see para. 5-14) under the heading "House of Commons: Minutes of Proceedings" (until 1975) or "Standing Committee . . ." (1976–date);

(iv) *Report stage* – if the **Bill** has been amended by the standing committee, this stage gives the House an opportunity to consider the changes. If necessary, the **Bill** may be referred back to the committee.

(v) *third reading* – after less detailed discussion at this stage, the **Bill** is passed to the House of Lords for its approval.

(vi) *Lords stage* – the **Bill** is reprinted when it is passed to the Lords for their approval. If the Lords make any amendments, these are referred back to the Commons for their approval. Only when both Houses are in agreement on the text can the **Bill** normally receive the Royal Assent.

Any **Bill** which does not pass through all these stages before the Parliamentary session ends fails, and a new **Bill** must be introduced at the beginning of the next session if legislation is to ensue.

5-8. CITATION OF BILLS

Every **Bill** submitted to Parliament (except **Bills** introduced by private members, which are only available from the Member of Parliament) is printed and placed on sale to the public by HMSO as soon as it receives its first reading. The printed **Bill** is given a number, which appears in the bottom left hand corner of the first page. If the number is printed enclosed in square brackets, this indicates that the **Bill** is a House of Commons **Bill**, *i.e.* it is at present being considered by the House of Commons. If the number is enclosed in round brackets, this indicates a **Bill** which is at present under consideration by the House of Lords. It is important to notice whether round or square brackets are used, as this will enable you to trace the correct **Bill**. The initials H.C. or H.L. are used to indicate the two different Houses of Parliament, and the parliamentary session is also given, as without this it is impossible to trace the **Bill**. A citation to a **Bill** should therefore give: the initials of the House; the session of Parliament; the **Bill** number in round (Lords) or square [Commons] brackets, *e.g.* H.L. **Bill** 1975–76 (10) Divorce (Scotland) Bill; H.C. **Bill** 1975–76 [10] Police Bill. When Parliament discusses the **Bill** they may incorporate some amendments. If these are only minor amendments, this is done by issuing a sheet of paper stating the amended version of the text. This bears the same number as the original **Bill**, but with the addition of a lower case letter, *e.g.* (38a). If a major alteration is made, the complete text of the **Bill** is reprinted, and this reprinted version is given a completely new number. If there have been a number of amendments, a marshalled list of amendments may be published, which also bears the same number as the original **Bill**, but with the addition of a roman number, *e.g.* [123 II].

Most **Bills** require the approval of both Houses of Parliament, and in this case it is again reprinted, with a new number, when it is passed to the other House for approval. Thus there may be several versions of the same **Bill** in the library, and it is often important that you should consult the latest copy, which incorporates all the amendments. You will find an explanation of how to trace the number of a **Bill** later in this Chapter (see para. 5-16).

At the end of each session a *Return of the Number of Public Bills* is published (as a House of Commons paper), showing which **Bills** considered during the session received the royal assent, and which were dropped, postponed or rejected.

Some idea of the progress of one **Bill** through both Houses of Parliament may be gained from the following example:

Unfair Contract Terms Bill (formerly the Avoidance of Liability (England and Wales) Bill) Session 1976/77
H.C. [98] [160] [184]
H.L. (155) (186) (215) (251)

5-9.   *Acts of Parliament*

These have been discussed in Chapter 3.

5-10.   *Papers of the House of Lords and House of Commons*

The House of Lords Papers and Bills are issued in a common numerical sequence, so that Papers and Bills are intermingled. The number of each item is printed in round brackets at the foot of the front cover. The citation is: H.L. session/paper number, *e.g.* H.L. 1975–76 (123).

The House of Commons Papers are issued in a separate numerical sequence from the Commons Bills. The citation includes the initials H.C., the session, and the paper number. The Papers of the House of Commons include reports of some committees, together with accounts, statistics and some annual reports which are required by Parliament for its work.

5-11.   *Parliamentary Debates*

The first semi-official reports of Parliament's debates were published in 1803 by William Cobbett. The man whose name is so strongly linked with the publication, Hansard, was a subsequent printer of the reports. There have been five series of **Parliamentary Debates**, *i.e.* first series, 1803–20; second series, 1820–30; third series, 1830–91; fourth series, 1892–1908; fifth series, 1909–date. Since 1909 the **Official Reports of Parliamentary Debates** have

been published by the House of Commons itself. The House of
Lords Debates have been published separately since 1909.
Previously, both Lords and Commons debates were published
together.

The **Official Report of Debates** is published daily and the
daily issues are later replaced by volumes containing reports of the
Debates during a Parliamentary session, with a sessional index. A
Weekly Hansard (containing all the daily reports, in one issue) is
also published, and a **Weekly Index** to the Debates is also
available.

Citations to Debates usually give the volume number/
House/series/date/column number. Each column (rather than each
page) is numbered, and references in the index are to column
numbers, not page numbers. If the number is printed in *italic*
type, this is a reference to the written answers which are in a
separate sequence at the back of the volume, and not to the column
in the Debates which bears that number. Entries in the index are
under the names of speakers, as well as under subjects. The first
issue of **Hansard** for each session contains a list of all members of
the House of Commons, and members of the Government are
listed in each volume of **Hansard**.

5-12.   NON-PARLIAMENTARY PUBLICATIONS

These are publications which are not presented to Parliament. They
include statutory instruments (para. 3-24). In most libraries these
publications are entered in the library catalogues, normally under
the heading "GREAT BRITAIN", followed by the name of the
government department which produced the publication, *e.g.*
GREAT BRITAIN. *Lord Chancellor's Office*. Many, but not all, of
these government reports are published by HMSO. They are
usually scattered around the library according to the subject matter
of the report rather than being kept together as a separate
collection.

5-13.   TRACING GOVERNMENT PUBLICATIONS

5-14.   *Indexes*

A **Daily List of Government Publications** is produced, and this is most useful for tracing very recent copies of Acts and other government publications. It is divided into parliamentary publications (House of Lords and Commons Papers and Bills, Command Papers, Acts and Debates), and non-parliamentary publications (arranged by the government department producing the report), including statutory instruments. There is also a list of publications by bodies such as the EEC, UN, and WHO, whose publications are sold, but not published, by HMSO. The *Daily List* is replaced (several months later) by a monthly catalogue entitled **Government Publications** of (month, year).

The monthly catalogue contains lists of House of Lords and House of Commons Papers and Bills arranged in number order; a list of Command Papers in numerical order (which can be used to trace the title of publications, if you only have the command number); and a list of Acts published during that month. The second part of the catalogue consists of a list of both parliamentary and non-parliamentary publications (excluding Bills, Acts and Debates, which appear only in the first part of the catalogue). This list is arranged by government departments and includes all items published by each department during that month with details of their prices, and the Command numbers, or Lords or Commons Paper numbers (in the case of parliamentary papers). Where the name of the Ministry began with the words "Ministry" or "Department," the entry has, until recently, been inverted, *e.g.* Environment, Department of. An index includes entries under subjects, titles, and the names of authors and chairmen. Statutory instruments are excluded – a separate monthly index is published (para. 3-27). The monthly issues are replaced by an annual catalogue, entitled **Government Publications 19--**. Every five years a consolidated index is published, *e.g.* 1961–65, 1966–70, 1971–75. In many libraries the catalogues for these years are bound together. To allow for this, the pagination of the catalogues is continuous over the five year period.

The annual and five yearly catalogues contain:
(1) Lists of parliamentary publications, arranged by session and then in numerical order by Bill numbers, Paper numbers and Command Paper numbers.
(2) A classified list of both parliamentary and non-

parliamentary publications (excluding Bills, Acts and Debates, which appear only in the first list). The list is arranged by the name of the government department which produced the publication, and full details of prices, command numbers, *etc.* are given.

(3) A list of periodicals, published by HMSO with prices.

(4) An alphabetical index, with entries under titles, subjects, and the names of authors and chairmen of committees. Statutory instruments are not included but a separate annual catalogue of statutory instruments is published (see para. 3-27).

Indexes covering longer periods are also available. There is a **General Alphabetical Index to the Bills, Reports and Papers printed by Order of the House of Commons and to the Reports and Papers presented by Command,** covering a ten year period, *e.g.* 1950–59, (session 1962–63, H.C. 96) and a **General Index 1900–1949.** Indexes and breviates (summaries) of nineteenth century papers also exist.

5-15.   *How to Trace a Command Paper*

If the number is known, note the spelling of the abbreviation for the word "Command" (see para. 5-5) as this will give you some idea of the date of the report. Cmnd. means that the publication was issued in or after 1956. Cmd. denotes a paper published before 1956. If the library binds its Parliamentary Publications into sessional sets (para. 5-2) consult the list in *Pemberton* (para. 5-5) to discover the session in which the report was published. You can then trace the appropriate volume in the sessional set by consulting the sessional index (para. 5-5). Full details of the title, *etc.* can also be found in the annual catalogue of government publications for the appropriate year (para. 5-14).

5-16.   *Tracing Bills*

5-17.   RECENT BILLS

The number(s) assigned to a recent Bill, and any amendments, can be found by using the **Daily List of Government Publications.** The progress of a Bill can be checked in the coloured pages printed weekly in the **New Law Journal** or in **Current Law** (under the heading "Parliament"). Bills published a few months ago can be traced in the monthly and annual catalogues of government publications (para. 5-14), which replace the *Daily List*.

The House of Commons Bills will be shelved together. In the case of House of Lords Bills, these may be interfiled with the House of Lords papers, for both the papers and the Bills share the same numerical sequence.

Debates on the Bill which take place at the committee stage (see para. 5-7) may be found in the **Official Reports of Standing Committees**. Debates in the House are reported in **Hansard** (paras. 5-11 and 5-21). When a Bill receives the Royal Assent this will be noted in publications such as the *New Law Journal* and *Current Law*. When the Royal Assent is given, a copy of the Act is printed, and an entry for the Act appears in the *Daily List*.

5-18. TRACING OLDER BILLS

It will seldom be necessary to refer to Bills from earlier sessions, for they will either have become law (in which case you should consult the resultant Act) or they will have lapsed. However, if you do need to consult older Bills, and your library has the bound sessional sets available, the text of all the versions of the Bill, together with all amendments, will be found, in alphabetical order, in the volumes entitled "Bills" at the beginning of the sessional set. If the bound volumes are not available, details of all the published versions of the Bill will be found at the beginning of the annual catalogues of **Government Publications**.

5-19. *Tracing Lords and Commons Papers*

If you have the paper number, the citation (para. 5-10) should include the session, the paper number, and whether it relates to the Lords or the Commons. If the library has bound the papers into sessional sets, the appropriate volume and page can be traced from the index to the session.

5-20. *Tracing Reports if You Know the Chairman*

If you know only the chairman of the report but lack further details (except possibly some idea of the subject matter) you should consult:

> S. Richard, *British Government Publications: An Index to Chairmen and Authors, 1900–1940*;
>
> A. M. Morgan, *British Government Publications; An Index to Chairmen and Authors, 1941–1966*;
>
> *Index to Chairmen of Committees, etc.* (published quarterly by HMSO);
>
> *Where to Look for Your Law* (1962 ed.).

If not traced in these publications, it will be necessary to consult the annual (or, if recent, the monthly) catalogues of government publications – these include entries under chairmen in their indexes.

5-21.   *Tracing Parliamentary Debates*

The last bound volume of the **Parliamentary Debates** for each session contains an Index. Discussions on a Bill are entered under the name of the Bill. The abbreviations 1R, 2R, 3R indicate the first, second and third readings. There are entries under subjects and under the names of Members. Entries give the volume number, in square brackets, and the column number (not the page number). Column numbers in *italic* type refer to the written answers which are printed separately at the back of each volume.

PROBLEMS

(a) In the 1974/75 session of Parliament, there was a Road Traffic (Seat Belts) Bill. How many readings had it received by the end of the session?

(b) In the 1974/75 session of Parliament a question was asked on the Development of Tourism Act. Find the question and the answer. Who answered the question?

(c) In the 1974/75 session, there was a question in the Commons on newspaper reports of proceedings in Juvenile Courts (look under "Juvenile Courts").

Give the volume and column numbers at which the debate appeared. Who asked the question?

Mr. Lyon, in answering, stated that in the circumstances outlined by the questioner, the disclosure of the information would be a breach of the Children and Young Persons Act 1933, s.49. To what information was he referring?

Indexes to the House of Commons and House of Lords debates are also published weekly, as part of (but issued separately from) **Weekly Hansard**. The arrangement is the same as the indexes to the sessional volumes.

5-22   *Tracing Publications on a Subject*

Parliamentary and non-parliamentary publications on a subject can be traced in the daily, monthly, annual and five-yearly catalogues of **Government Publications** (see para. 5-14), and in the **General Indexes** 1900–1949, 1950–1959 (see para. 5-14). If bound sessional sets are available, the sessional indexes may be used as an alternative to consulting the annual catalogues. A series of **Sectional Lists** cover the publications which have been produced by a particular government department, *e.g.* the Home Office, and which are still in print (*i.e.* still available for purchase from HMSO). These may serve as a form of subject index. If your library shelves its non-parliamentary publications by subject, the library's subject catalogue will enable you to trace relevant publications.

5-23.   *Tracing Statutes, Statutory Instruments, Treaties*

The **Chronological Table of the Statutes** (para 6-24) and **Index to the Statutes** (para. 6-18) can be used to trace Acts, and a separate annual list of statutes is also published (para. 6-24). Statutory instruments are traced through the **Daily List** and through monthly and annual **Lists of Statutory Instruments** (paras. 6-28, 6-30). Chronological and alphabetical indexes are also available. Treaties are included in the daily, monthly and annual government catalogues. In addition there are separate annual and 3 to 4 yearly **Indexes to the Treaty Series** (para. 8-4) and a consolidated **Index of British Treaties** 1101–1968 (para. 8-5). There is a sectional list (list giving all Treaty series from 1919–date). For more detailed discussion on these topics, see paras. 6-16, 6-26, 8-5.

5-24.   *Law Commission Reports and Working Papers*

Some of the **Law Commission reports** are published as Command Papers, others are House of Commons papers, whilst many more are non-parliamentary papers. As a result, they may be widely scattered in the library. In many law libraries they will be kept together and may be available only from a member of the library staff. Every report and working paper has its own individual number within the series. A complete list of all the reports and working papers which have been published is given in every copy of the **Law Commission's Annual Report** (issued as a House of Commons paper). The list gives the Command number or paper numbers, where relevant, and indicates, for each report, whether the Commission's proposals for reform have been implemented and, if so, by what statute this was done. Law Commission reports appear in the monthly and annual catalogues of government publications in the classified section (under "Lord Chancellor's Office").

5-25.   AVAILABILITY OF PARLIAMENTARY PAPERS

Older parliamentary papers may be available on microfilm or in the form of reprints published by the Irish University Press. (These reprints are arranged in subject order). It may be possible to trace a summary of a report in the *Breviates of Parliamentary Papers*, produced by P. & G. Ford. Copies of material which is still in print may be purchased from any branch of HMSO (addresses appear on the *Daily List* and in the monthly and annual catalogue) or through any bookseller. Photocopies of out of print publications can be purchased. The current cost of new publications is given in the HMSO catalogues. Publications may also be available on loan through the inter-library loan service.

PROBLEMS

(a)   What is the title of Cmnd. 6148 published in 1975?

(b)   Find the number of the British Summer Time Bill. Was it a Lords or a Commons Bill? In what session of Parliament was it discussed? Use the Consolidated Index to Government Publications 1971–75.

(c)   Use *Government Publications 1974* to locate the Phillimore Report. What is the subject of the Report?

(d)   Give the Command number.

(e)   Using the latest Annual Report of the Law Commission, or *Government Publications 1974*, give the number of the Law Commission Report on Injuries to Unborn Children.

(f)   Use the latest Annual Report of the Law Commission to check if the recommendations on the report have been implemented – if so, by what Act?

(g)   A report on Bail Procedures in Magistrates' Courts was published in 1974. Which government department produced the report?

Chapter 6

HOW TO FIND INFORMATION ON A SUBJECT

6-1.   INTRODUCTION

One of the most difficult tasks facing you will be to discover the law relating to a particular topic. Invariably your essays, moots and seminar preparation will require you to know not simply the present state of the law but also its development and such criticisms and suggestions for reform as have been made.

To find information on a subject you will need to consult some or all of the following sources:

Acts of Parliament
Delegated legislation
Cases
Textbooks
Periodical articles
Relevant government publications, including Law Commission
    Reports (especially those which have made suggestions for
    reform of the law)
Reports and comments in newspapers
Bills and Parliamentary Debates

In order to tackle a legal problem you may need to ask yourself the following questions:
Question: Where can I find a general statement of the law on this subject?
Answer: In encyclopedias, such as *Halsbury's Laws of England* (para. 6-2) and in textbooks.
Question: What books are there on this subject?
Answer: Consult the library catalogues (para. 1-4) and bibliographies (para. 6-33).
Question: What periodical articles have been written on this subject?
Answer: Consult indexes to periodicals (para. 4-2).
Question: What cases have there been on this topic?
Answer: Use digests and indexes to case law (para. 6-8).

Question: What judicial interpretation has been placed on particular words?

Answer: Look in *Words and Phrases Legally Defined* (para. 6-15) and similar works (para. 6-15).

Question: What Acts of Parliament are in force dealing with this subject?

Answer: Use *Statutes in Force,* (para. 6-17), *Halsbury's Statutes* (para. 6-19), or the *Index to the Statutes* (para. 6-18).

Question: Are there any relevant statutory instruments?

Answer: Use *Index to Government Orders* (para. 6-28), *Lists of Statutory Instruments* (para. 6-29), or *Halsbury's Statutory Instruments* (para. 6-27).

Question: Have there been any government reports or Law Commission reports on this topic?

Answer: Use indexes to government publications (para. 5-14) and the annual reports of the Law Commission (para. 5-24).

Question: Are there any Bills before Parliament which would change the law on this subject? Has the issue been discussed in Parliament?

Answer: Consult indexes to government publications (para. 5-14) and Parliamentary Debates (paras. 5-11, 5-21).

Having mapped out the ground, you can now proceed to tackle these questions. In attempting to carry out a search on a legal subject you may have some difficulty. Never be afraid to ask the library staff or your lecturer for help. Remember that other students may also be working on the same subject — start work well within the time limits set, otherwise you may discover that the material is unavailable because of high demand.

6-2.   LEGAL ENCYCLOPEDIAS

These contain a detailed up-to-date statement of the law on a particular subject. The major general legal encyclopedia is **Halsbury's Laws of England**, which is now in its fourth edition. It is a most important source of information and you will need to refer to it throughout your course of study. Some of the volumes of the fourth edition have not yet been published, and so, for some subjects, it will still be necessary for you to use the third edition, which is kept up-to-date by supplementary volumes.

6-3.   *How to Use Halsbury's Laws of England*

The entries are alphabetically arranged, using fairly general subject headings, *e.g.* "Divorce," "Education." The arrangement of the third and fourth editions differs slightly, and as you must still consult the third edition if the relevant material has not yet been included in the fourth edition, you must understand the arrangement of both editions.

6-4.   HOW TO USE THE THIRD EDITION

1. Look up the subject in the General Index (Volumes 41 to 42). The figure printed in **bold** type is the volume number which contains the relevant material, and the figure in ordinary type is the page number within that volume, *e.g.*

RUG
  beating in street, offence of, **33**, 612.

2. Turn to the appropriate volume and page number. Entries are alphabetically arranged under broad subjects, and each subject is then further subdivided, covering different aspects of the topic. A list of references to related subject headings is given at the beginning of each subject. Before consulting the entry check in the *Index Key to the Fourth Edition* (para. 6-5) to see if that particular subject has been covered in the fourth edition. If so, use the fourth edition.

3. Every paragraph has an individual number. The main body of the text contains a statement of the law on a particular topic and the footnotes (in smaller type) provide the authority for the statement; that is, they provide a list of the relevant statutes, statutory instruments and cases which have established that point of law. There is a detailed subject index at the back of each volume.

4. Make a note of the volume and paragraph number(s) which contain the information you require. Now turn to the *Cumulative Supplement*. This shows any amendments, volume by volume, and paragraph by paragraph, to the text printed in the main work.

Look under the volume and paragraph numbers which you have noted. If there has been any change in the law since the main volume was published it will be shown here, together with the more recent cases on the same subject.

5. Finally, look in the looseleaf *Current Service* volume, at the section headed "Key." This consists of a list of volume numbers and paragraph numbers. Look to see whether the volume number and paragraph numbers which you noted appear on this list. If there is an entry for your volume and paragraph there has been a change in the law during the last few months.

6. Note the key number (a combination of letters and numbers) printed beside your entry. Look at the bottom of the page. This will tell you whether the entry you require is to be found in the *Monthly Reviews* (which are at the front of the *Current Service* volume) or in the *Noter-up* (at the back of the volume, immediately after the *Key* which you are at present consulting). Find the relevant entry, and any change in the law during the last few months is shown.

7. If you suspect that there has been a recent change in the law, you can consult the *Index* in the *Current Service* volume. This is a cumulative subject index to the contents of the *Monthly Reviews* (which are at the beginning of the volume). The letters and numbers given after each subject refer you to the relevant entries in the Reviews section.

In order to be certain that you have missed nothing, it is essential that you should work systematically through the sequence outlined above, *i.e.* main work; cumulative supplement; current service volume.

When all three have been checked you will know that your information is up-to-date to within a few weeks of the present day. If you are looking for a relatively new topic, which you are unable to trace in the general index (*e.g.* hi-jacking, hoax bombs, hovercraft), look in the *Index* to the supplement, printed at the back of the *Cumulative Supplement*. This will refer you to a volume and paragraph. Look in the *Cumulative Supplement* under that volume and paragraph to locate the relevant information, *e.g.*

hoax bombs, 11, 1205.

This entry in the *Cumulative Supplement* to the fourth edition refers you to the entry in the *Cumulative Supplement* for Volume 11, paragraph 1205, where the law relating to hoax bombs is set out.

6-5. HOW TO USE THE FOURTH EDITION

The fourth edition of **Halsbury's Laws** commenced publication in 1973, and more than 20 volumes have been published, covering the first part of the alphabet. Entries are arranged alphabetically by subject, *e.g.* Volume 8 contains "Compulsory Acquisition to Constitutional Law." Although, in general, the headings used are the same as those in the third edition, there have been some alterations. For instance, the topics treated in the third edition under the heading "Aliens and Nationality" are now dealt with under the heading "British Nationality."

1. If you have the third edition available, you can use the index to that edition (Volumes 41 to 42) to find out which volume deals with your subject. Having traced the information in the appropriate volume of the third edition, turn to the *Index Key to the Fourth Edition* which is printed at the back of the *Cumulative Supplement* to the fourth edition. This will tell you whether the information in this volume has been replaced by a fourth edition volume.

2. Let us suppose that you are interested in the law relating to gambling. From the index to the third edition (Volume 41) you discover that this topic is in Volume 18 of the third edition. On looking at Volume 18, you find that this is dealt with under the heading "Gaming and Wagering." You now need to check whether the information on gaming and wagering in this volume has been replaced by more recent information in the fourth edition. If you look in the *Cumulative Supplement* to the third and fourth editions, or to the fourth edition (two cumulative supplements are published and your library may have either), at the back of the part of the

supplement dealing with the fourth edition you will find an *"Index Key to the Fourth Edition."* Part of the entry for Volume 18 from this Index Key is reproduced below:

Third Edition Volume and Page **Volume 18**	*Fourth Edition* Title and Volume
1-115 Friendly Societies	Friendly Societies, Vol. 19
117-166 Game	Animals, Vol. 2
167-248 Gaming and Wagering	Betting, Gaming and Lotteries, Vol. 4.

This indicates that you will find more up to date information on gambling in the fourth edition, under the new heading "Betting, gaming and lotteries," which appears in Volume 4.

3. Once you know which volume of the fourth edition you need to consult, you can use the detailed subject index which appears at the back of each volume to locate the exact paragraph number which contains the information you need. (Entries in the indexes to the fourth edition refer to paragraph numbers, not to page numbers). The volumes contain separate subject indexes for each subject covered in that volume; thus, in Volume 4, there are separate alphabetical indexes at the back of the volume for Betting, Bills of Exchange, Bills of Sale, and all the other subjects dealt with in that volume.

4. An index to the first ten volumes of the fourth edition of **Halsbury's Laws** has been published, covering A − Cremation. (This will be replaced by an index to Volumes 1 to 20). Entries give the volume number, in **bold** type, and the paragraph number. Cross-references are provided from one heading to another, *e.g.*

CREMATION.
    authorities. *See* BURIAL
    AUTHORITY.

The individual volumes of the fourth edition contain tables (lists) of the statutes, statutory instruments and cases referred to in that volume.

5. It is essential, once you have located the relevant entry, that you check that the information given is still correct. This is done by looking in the *Cumulative Supplement* to the fourth edition (or the third and fourth editions) under the volume number and paragraph number which you consulted in the main work. Any changes will be noted here.

6. Finally, you should look in the looseleaf *Current Service* volume, at the part marked *Key*. If your volume and paragraph number appears here, there has been a recent change or amendment, details of which are contained in the looseleaf volume (para. 6-4).

The *Monthly Reviews* (filed in the *Current Service* volume) can also be used as a general means of keeping up with new developments in the subjects you are studying, since they give recent changes in the law. Entries are arranged in subject order. The monthly copies are replaced by an *Annual Abridgement* which is also arranged by subject, and which summarises all the changes in the law during a particular year. At the beginning of each subject heading in the *Abridgement* is a list of periodical articles written on that topic during the year. The *Abridgements* were first published in 1974.

HOW TO USE HALSBURY'S LAWS OF ENGLAND IF BOTH THE THIRD AND FOURTH EDITIONS ARE AVAILABLE

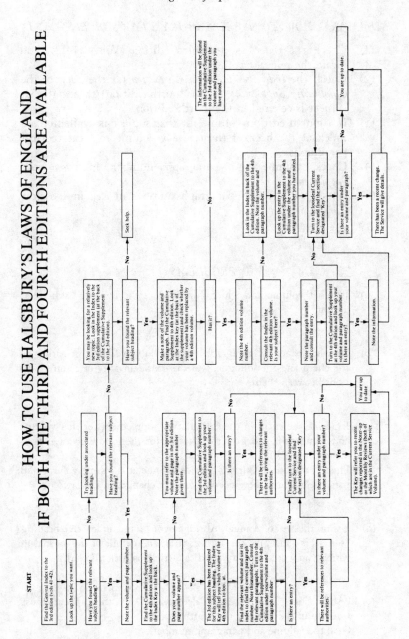

SUMMARY: HOW TO USE HALSBURY'S LAWS OF ENGLAND

(1) Check the *Index* to the third edition (Vols. 41-42), and locate the relevant volume.

(2) Check the *Index key to the fourth edition* (at the back of the *Cumulative Supplement* to the fourth edition) to see if that subject is covered in the fourth edition.

(3) If a fourth edition volume for that subject is available, use index at the back of the relevant volume to locate correct paragraphs.

(4) Check volume and paragraph number in *Cumulative Supplement*.

(5) Check volume and paragraph number in *Key* in looseleaf *Current Service* volume.

PROBLEMS

(a) In what volume and which edition does the heading "solicitors" appear?

(b) At what page and paragraph number do you find information on the client and the solicitor, and the confidentiality of communications between them?

(c) Examine the entry in the Cumulative Supplement for that volume and paragraph, and give the citation for the following case: *R* v. *Barton*.
Finally, check the Current Service volume at the same volume and paragraph. Have there been any recent changes in the law?

(d) Using the 1976 Annual Abridgement, look under the heading "solicitors" and give the author, title, and details of the journal in which you would find a periodical article on articled clerks.

(e) "Abduction, consent, as a defence". Does this appear most recently in the third or the fourth edition?
Give the volume and paragraph number.

(f) You are asked to check what is the statute law on "Animals," the import restrictions of rare animals" (use the fourth edition, Volume 2). Is the Animals (Restriction of Importation) Act 1964 still in force?
If not, what replaced it?

(g) You are trying to trace a statement of the law relating to bonds, which appears in Volume 3 of the third edition, at pages 329–351. In what volume of the fourth edition is this subject dealt with, and under what heading?

(h) Volume 2 of the fourth edition, at paragraph 414, deals with the subject of captive birds. Has there been any change in the law since this paragraph was written?
If so, what are the changes?

6-6.   *Specialised Encyclopedias*

There are a number of specialised encyclopedias which can provide you with an up-to-date statement of the law in particular subject areas. Many of these are issued in looseleaf format, so that the information can be up-dated by the insertion of replacement pages whenever there is a change in the law. One important series, published by Sweet and Maxwell, covers such topics as Housing, Planning, Public Health, Compulsory Purchase and Compensation, and Value Added Tax. A number of other publishers have issued similar works. Looseleaf encyclopedias are particularly useful in subjects such as taxation, where the law changes very rapidly. Before using a looseleaf encyclopedia you should check the pages near the beginning of the volume which tell you how recent the information is. This will enable you to be certain that the latest supplementary pages have all been inserted. Looseleaf encyclopedias usually contain an explanation of the law, together with the up-to-date versions of the relevant statutes, statutory instruments and government circulars, and notes of all relevant cases. Publishers are now issuing some textbooks in conjunction with a looseleaf volume, so that the book can be kept completely up-to-date. This is a development of the long-established practice of issuing cumulative supplements in between editions, to modernise the last edition.

6-7.   *Precedent Books and Rule Books*

These are essentially intended for the practitioner. The basic object of precedent books is to provide specimens of wills, conveyances, tenancy agreements and the other forms of legal documents which solicitors are called upon to draw up. In addition, there are some precedent books which provide specimens of the types of forms which will be required whenever a case is taken to court. Rule books contain the rules which govern procedure in court, and specimen copies of the various orders and forms used by the courts, and by the parties to litigation.

The **Encyclopaedia of Forms and Precedents** aims to provide a form for every transaction likely to be encountered by practitioners, except for court forms. The entries are arranged by subject, *e.g.* Animals, Mortgages. Some idea of the wide scope of the work can be obtained by glancing through the subject headings. For instance, the section on animals covers such diverse topics as the sale and leasing of animals, applications for licences to keep a bull, or to keep an animals' boarding establishment, a veterinary surgeon's certificate for the destruction of an animal, and the relevant documents prohibiting movement of animals during an outbreak of disease. A cumulative noter-up and two looseleaf service volumes keep the text of the main work up-to-date, and provide new precedents. **Atkin's Encyclopaedia of Court Forms in Civil Proceedings** is a complementary publication, covering the procedure in civil courts and tribunals. The volume on divorce, for instance, contains all the necessary documents needed during the court action, together with a detailed list of the steps to be taken and the forms required at each stage. The volumes are re-issued from time to time to incorporate new material. An annual supplement and a half-yearly service booklet keep the information up-to-date.

Precedents for the Conveyancer (issued as a supplement to the journal *The Conveyancer*) is an example of a more specialised precedent book.

The rules and procedures governing various courts are set out in a number of places. The **County Court Practice**, and the **Supreme Court Practice** (often referred to as the "White Book") set out the documents required for those appearing in those courts. **Archbold's Criminal Pleading, Evidence and Practice** is used by those engaged in criminal work. Some practitioners' textbooks will include precedents; these can be traced through the library's subject catalogue.

The coloured pages in each issue of the *New Law Journal* are of particular interest to practitioners. These often include specimen forms and precedents, and details of Home Office circulars and practice directions. Practice directions are also published in the major series of law reports, *e.g. All England Law Reports, Weekly Law Reports*.

6-8.   TRACING CASES ON A SUBJECT

Cases on a particular subject can be traced by consulting:
  Current Law;
  Current Law Year Books;
  English and Empire Digest;
  Halsbury's Laws of England;
  Indexes and digests to individual series of law reports, *e.g. Law
    Reports Indexes, Consolidated Tables and Index to the All England
    Law Reports*;
  Relevant textbooks and periodical articles.

6-9.   *How to use Current Law*

Current Law is published monthly, and claims to cover "all the law from every source." It is an important publication and it is essential that you should learn how to use it. Read the pamphlet *How to use Current Law*, which should be available in the library.

The main part of each monthly issue is arranged by subject and under each subject heading is given a summary of: recent cases on the subject; new statutes and statutory instruments; government reports and recent periodical articles on that subject. Full details are given to enable you to trace the cases and other materials mentioned in your own library.

At the front of each issue is a *Cumulative Case Citator*, which contains a list of all the cases which have been reported during the current year. It is therefore only necessary to look in the latest issue of **Current Law** to trace a case reported at any time during the year. (This list of cases brings the information in the *Current Law Citators* (paras. 2-14, 2-17) up-to-date).

The monthly issues also contain a *subject index*. Again, it is only necessary to consult the index in the latest month's issue of **Current Law**. This enables you to trace any development in the law during the current year. The reference given, *e.g.* Contract, Jan 24 is to the appropriate monthly issue of **Current Law** (in this example, the January issue). Every item in each issue has its own individual number; the item you require in the January issue is number 24, and there you will find a recent case, or some other development in the law of contract summarised. The subject index naturally increases in size during the year. As more new topics are included you will find that part of the index is printed at the front of the monthly issue and part of it is at the back of the issue. If your library possesses the Scottish edition of **Current Law** (which has a green cover), the pages printed on green paper in the centre of the issue (and which have a higher series of item numbers than the remainder of the issue) relate to changes in Scottish law.

A list of new periodical articles is printed under each subject heading. On the back cover of each monthly issue is a list of newly published law books.

As we have already seen (para. 2-14) the *Current Law Citators* provide you with a list of reports for a case. This information can be brought up-to-date for the current year by looking at the list of cases in the latest issue of **Current Law**. Suppose, however, that you know that there has been a recent case on the subject but you do not know the name of the parties. In this instance you can trace the cases on that subject during the current year by looking in the cumulative subject index in the latest issue of **Current Law**. If you have spelt the name of the parties incorrectly, or have an incomplete reference, you can trace the case by the subject approach, using the subject index to **Current Law**.

6-10.   *How to Use Current Law Year Books*

The monthly issues of **Current Law** are replaced by an annual volume, the **Current Law Year Book**. (Your library may possess the Scottish version, the **Scottish Current Law Year Book**. Despite the name, this includes all the English materials, plus a separate section at the back of the volume containing Scottish developments during the year).

The Year Book is arranged by subject, in the same way as the monthly issues, and contains a summary of all the cases, legislation and other developments in that subject during the year. (As noted above, developments in Scottish law are printed in a separate sequence at the back of the **Scottish Current Law Year Book**). A list of periodical articles written on a subject during the year is printed at the back of the volume. (The 1956 **Year Book** contains a list of periodical articles published between 1947 and 1956). A list of the books published during the year, also arranged by subject, appears at the back of the volume.

The 1976 **Year Book** contains, at the back, *a subject index to all the entries in all the Year Books from 1947–1976*. Entries give the last two digits of the year, and a reference to the individual item number within that year's volume, *e.g.* 69/3260 is a reference to item 3260 in the 1969 **Year Book**. Entries which have no year in front of them will be found in the **Current Law Consolidation 1947–1951**. A new subject index for all entries in all the **Year Books** published after 1971 began in 1977. The entry in the latest **Year Book** should therefore be consulted, together with the entry in the 1976 **Year Book**, and the latest monthly issue of **Current Law**. These three sources will provide complete coverage of any developments in the law of that subject since 1947.

Master Volumes were published in the 1956, 1961, 1966 and 1971 **Year Books**. These volumes contain, under the usual subject headings, detailed entries for all developments during the year in which they were published, together with a summary of the developments during the previous four years. References are given to enable you to trace the full details in the appropriate **Current Law Year Book**. Thus, it is possible, by using the **Master Volumes** and the **Current Law Consolidation 1947–1951**, to see at a glance every entry which has appeared in **Current Law** on a particular subject over a five year period. For instance, the 1971 **Year Book** prints in full the details of all cases, legislation, etc. which took place during 1971, together with summaries of all

developments in that subject during 1967–1970. The location of
the full details of each case, etc., in the 1967, 1968, 1969 and
1970 **Year Books** is given. The **Master Volumes** therefore enable
you to survey the developments in the law of a particular subject
over a five year period, in more detail than is possible in the
subject index.

SUMMARY: HOW TO USE CURRENT LAW

(1) To trace a specific case, of which you know the name, in
order to discover where it is reported, and whether the case
has subsequently been judicially considered, consult:
Current Law Case Citator 1947–1976 *and*
Current Law Citator *and*
List of cases in the latest monthly issue of **Current
Law**.

(2) To trace any developments (cases, statutes, etc.) on a
particular subject, consult:
the Index 1947–1976 at the back of the 1976 **Year
Book** *and*
the index at the back of the latest **Year Book** *and*
the subject index in the latest monthly issue of
Current Law.

(3) To obtain a general view of developments in a topic over a
number of years, consult:
Current Law Consolidation 1947–1951 *and*
Master Volumes (1956, 1961, 1966 and 1971 **Year
Books**) *and*
all the **Year Books** published since the last Master
Volume was issued *and*
all the monthly issues of **Current Law** for this
year.

(4) To trace periodical articles on a subject look in the 1956
Year Book *and each* subsequent **Year Book**, and in the
monthly issues of **Current Law** (N.B. There are other
sources for tracing periodical articles: para. 4-2).

(5) To trace books published on a subject look in each **Year
Book** and on the back covers of the monthly issues of
Current Law (N.B. There are many other sources for
tracing books on a subject: para. 6-33).

Remember that **Current Law** only contains information on cases
reported or mentioned in court since 1947 and other developments

in the law since 1947. To trace earlier cases use the *English and Empire Digest* and to trace other developments in the law prior to 1947 use *Halsbury's Laws of England*.

PROBLEMS

(a) Name the cases reported between 1947–1977 on "Champerty and maintenance."

(b) Give the Law Report citation of the case on chance medley reported between 1947–1951.

(c) Under the heading "Criminal law" look up the subject "Hijacking," and name three developments in this subject since 1970.

6-11.   *The English and Empire Digest*

The **English and Empire Digest** contains summaries of cases which have appeared in law reports from the thirteenth century to the present day, arranged in subject order. It enables you to trace cases of any date which deal with your particular subject. In addition to English cases, reports of Irish, Scottish and many Commonwealth cases are included. These are printed in smaller type to enable them to be easily distinguished from English cases.

The arrangement is by subject using, as far as possible, similar headings to those in **Halsbury's Laws of England** and it is cross-referenced to that work. Each main subject heading is further subdivided, so as to bring together all the cases on a topic. Every entry has its own individual number. Those numbers relating to Commonwealth, Scottish and Irish cases are numbered in a different sequence to the English cases. A summary of the decision in every case is given, followed by the name of the case, and a list of places where the case is reported. The subsequent judicial history of the case is also shown, in annotations. A list of the abbreviations used for law reports will be found in the front of Volume 1 and also in the *Cumulative Supplement*.

6-12.   HOW TO USE THE ENGLISH AND EMPIRE DIGEST TO TRACE
CASES ON A SUBJECT

As has been explained, (para. 2-15), the **English and Empire Digest** is at present being re-issued. You will therefore find on the shelves some volumes with a blue band on the spine, and some (re-issued) volumes with a green band on the spine.

At the end of the main work, there are five volumes of indexes (Vols. 52 to 56), four *Continuation Volumes*, A, B, C and D (which cover new cases published between 1952 and 1975) and a *Cumulative Supplement* which brings the information in all the volumes up-to-date. Because the volumes are in the process of being re-issued, the use of the **English and Empire Digest** appears somewhat complicated.

Let us suppose that we wish to trace cases on contract, which relate to an offer made in an advertisement. If we turn to the *Consolidated Index* (Vols. 55 to 56) and look under the heading "Contract," we find the entry:

Contract
    advertisement —
        offer made by. *See* OFFER.

On looking up the entry under Offer we find:
    Offer
        advertisement, by, 12[a], 59[b], *321–325*[c]; 62[b], *333*[c]
    [a]Volume number.
    [b]Page number.
    [c]Case numbers.

Volume 12 has a green band across the spine. Since the index volumes (Vols. 52 to 56) have a blue band across them, the information contained in the indexes is correct for any volumes bearing a blue band. If the volumes have been re-issued and now have a green band across them, the page numbers may be different from those shown in the index. Since Volume 12 is a green band volume, we can assume that it is unlikely that our cases on advertisements will still appear on page 59. We should therefore turn to the back of Volume 12 where we will find both an index to the contents of that Volume and a *"Reference Adaptor."* We can look the subject up again in the index to Volume 12, and the entry will give us the new page number and case number, *e.g.*

Advertisement
    offer of indemnity establishing contract, 66, *342*

This tells us that the case we want will be found on page 66, and the relevant case is numbered 342. If the case has an asterisk (*) in front of the number, this indicates that it is an Irish, Scottish or Commonwealth case, and we must remember to look in the separate sequence of cases in smaller print for it.

If we do not want to go to the trouble of looking the subject up again in the index, we can use the *"Reference Adaptor"* at the back of the volume. The reference adaptor is in two sequences; one relating to English cases, the other to Commonwealth cases. If we look in the English case adaptor we find a list of the case numbers which were used in the blue band volumes (called here, rather confusingly, Replacement Volumes) and the new case number for the same case in the re-issued green band volume. You will remember that our entry was for case numbers 321 to 325. If we look at the Reference Adaptor at the back of Volume 12 we find the following entry:

Replacement Volume (*i.e.* blue band vols.)	Reissue Volume (*i.e.* green band vols.)
321	339
322	340
323	342
324	343
325	344

This means that our cases, which were formerly numbered 321–325, have now been renumbered 339–344. If we look through the volume, we will see the case numbers printed in square brackets at the top of the page. There are two series of case numbers at the top of each page; those preceded by an asterisk relate to Commonwealth cases, which are printed in smaller type, and which have a separate sequence of case numbers. Our cases, 339–343, are found on pages 66–67.

Had Volume 12 still had a blue band, our task would have been much easier. It would only have been necessary to turn to page 59, and to look for the cases numbered 321–325 on that page.

The information in the blue band volumes is now a number of years out of date. The green band volumes are more up to date (the actual date published is given at the front of each volume) but there are still likely to have been some changes, and some new cases, since the volumes were issued. It is therefore necessary to check that your information is still current. This is done by consulting the *Cumulative Supplement*. The *Continuation Volumes* A (1952–1963), B (1964–1966), C (1967–1970) and D (1971–1975) contain new cases on the various subjects dealt with in the main work. Thus *Continuation Volume* D contains all the new cases reported in the period 1971–1975 on all the subjects covered in the main work. The entries in the *Continuation Volumes* are arranged by subject, in exactly the same way as the main volumes.

The *Cumulative Supplement* brings the information in both the main work and the *Continuation Volumes* up to date, by noting additional cases on the same topic, referring to subsequent cases in which an earlier case has been judicially considered, etc. This information is contained in the front half of the *Cumulative Supplement* (called the *Noter-Up*). The back half of the supplement contains a summary, in subject order, of all the cases which have been reported since 1975, when the last *Continuation Volume* was published.

The *Noter-Up* (in the front half of the *Cumulative Supplement*) brings the information in both the blue band and the green band volumes up to date, and brings to your attention any additional cases which have appeared in the *Continuation Volumes* or in the back half of the *Cumulative Supplement* itself. The entries in the *Noter-Up* give you, volume by volume, and case by case, any amendments or changes. Brief extracts from the entry in the main volume and the *Noter-Up* relating to the entries for Volume 12 – Contract – may make this clear. (Illustrations V and VI, pp. 103, 104).

Part V.—Consideration

SECT. 1.   **IN GENERAL**

LAW.   *See* HALSBURY'S LAWS (3rd Edn.),
Vol. 8, pp. 113 *et seq.*
CROSS-REFERENCE.   *See* FRAUDULENT &
VOIDABLE CONVEYANCES, Vol. 25 (Repl.),
Nos. 108 *et seq.*

1393. Consideration.]—A consideration is a cause
or meritorious occasion requiring a mutual recompense in fact or in law. Contracts & bargains
have a *quid pro quo.*—CALTHORPE'S CASE (1574),
Dyer, 334 b ; 73 E. R. 756.
Annotations:—**Consd.** Magdalen College, Cambridge Case
(1615), 11 Co. Rep. 66 b ; *Wain v.* Warlters (1804), 5
East, 10.

1394. ——.]—HAMMON v. ROLL, No. 1403, *post.*

1395. ——.]—THOMAS v. THOMAS, No. 1560,
post.

1396. Good consideration.]—There are two manners of gifts on a good consideration, *scil.* consideration of nature or blood, & a valuable consideration.—TWYNE'S CASE (1602), 3 Co. Rep.
80 b.; Moore, K. B. 638 ; [1558–1774] All E. R. Rep.
302 ; 76 E. R. 809.
Annotations:—**Refd.** Bennet v. Musgrove (1750), 2 Ves. Sen.
51 ; Ryall v. Rowles (1750), 1 Ves. Sen. 348 ; Holbird v.
Anderson (1793), 5 Term Rep. 235 ; Kelson v. Kelson
(1853), 1 W. R. 143 ; Corlett v. Radcliffe (1860), 14
Moo. P. C. C. 121.

See, further, Nos. 1740, *et seq., post.*

1397. Valuable consideration.]—A valuable consideration, in the sense of the law, may consist
either in some right, interest, profit or benefit
accruing to the one party, or some forbearance,
detriment, loss or responsibility given, suffered or
undertaken by the other (*per* CUR.).—CURRIE v.
MISA (1875), L. R. 10 Exch. 153 ; 44 L. J. Ex. 94 ;
23 W. R. 450, Ex. Ch. ; *affd. sub nom.* MISA
v. CURRIE (1876), 1 App. Cas. 554 ; [1874–80] All
E. R. Rep. 686 ; 45 L. J. Q. B. 852 ; 35 L. T. 414 ;
24 W. R. 1049, H. L.
Annotations:—**Consd.** Fleming v. Bank of New Zealand,
[1900] A. C. 577 ; Ball v. National & Grindlays Bank, Ltd.,
[1971] 3 All E. R. 485. **Refd.** Jones v. Waring & Gillow,
[1926] A. C. 670 ; *Re* Cuthbert, *Ex p.* Momoyer British
Construction Co. v. Trustees, [1936] 1 All E. R. 342 ; Oliver
v. Davis, [1949] 2 All E. R. 353 ; Barclays Bank, Ltd.
v. Astley Industrial Trust, Ltd., [1970] 1 All E. R. 719.

SCOTTISH, IRISH AND COMMONWEALTH CASES

880. *Consideration.*]—The definition of " consideration "
in Indian Contract Act is wider than the requirement of the
English law.—DEBNARAYAN DUTT v. CHUNILAL GHOSE
(1913), I. L. R. 41 Calc. 137.—IND.
881. *Valuable consideration.*]—To constitute a valuable
consideration it is not necessary that it should be a money
consideration.—CROCKFORD v. EQUITABLE INSURANCE Co.
(1863), 5 All. 651.—CAN.
882. ——.]—There is no difference between the French
law, which prevails in Lower Canada, & the English law
on the subjects of the necessity of valuable consideration
for a contract.—MCGREEVY v. RUSSELL (1886), 56 L. T.
501.—CAN.
883. ——.]—To entitle a party to an agreement, other
than a donation, to sue thereon, the common law of the
Cape Colony requires that such party must have given some
quid pro quo or valuable consideration under the agreement.—
MIRABU v. WEBSTER (1899), 21 S. C. 323.—S. AF.
884. ——.]—A good cause of action can be founded on a
promise made seriously & deliberately & with the intention
that a lawful obligation should be established.—CONRADIE v.
ROUSSOUW, [1919] App. D. 279.—S. AF.

885. —— *Burden of proof.*]—Where an option states
that it is given " for value received " the *onus* of showing
there was in fact no consideration is upon the optionor.—
BISHOP v. GRAY, [1944] 4 D. L. R. 743 ; O. W. N. 700.—
CAN.

SECT. 2.   **NECESSITY FOR (NUDUM PACTUM).**

LAW.   *See* HALSBURY'S LAWS (3rd Edn.),
Vol. 8, p. 113.
CROSS-REFERENCES.   *See* Nos. 5357 *et seq.*,
post (novation of contract); Nos. 1403,
1758, *post* (promise to pay debt already
released); BILLS OF EXCHANGE, PROMISSORY NOTES & NEGOTIABLE INSTRUMENTS, Vol. 6 (Repl.), Nos. 813 *et seq.*;
GUARANTEE & INDEMNITY, Vol. 26
(Repl.), Nos. 56 *et seq.* (as requisite of
guarantee); DEEDS & OTHER INSTRUMENTS, Vol. 17 (Repl.), Nos. 12 *et seq.*,
& FRAUDULENT & VOIDABLE CONVEYANCES, Vol. 25 (Repl.), Nos. 226 *et seq.*
(necessity for consideration in deed).

1398. General rule.]—Where there is no consideration, *i.e.* upon *nudum pactum*, there ought
to be no more help in Chancery than there is at the
common law.—ANON. (prior to 1602), Cary, 5 ;
21 E. R. 3.

1399. ——.]—A. delivered £20 to B. to the use
of C., a woman, to be delivered her the day of her
marriage. Before her marriage A. countermanded
it, & called home the money:—*Held :* C. should
not be aided in Chancery, because there was no
consideration why she should have it.—LYTE v.
PENY (1541), 1 Dyer, 49 a ; 73 E. R. 108 ; *sub
nom.* ANON. Cary, 9.
Annotations:—**Refd.** Rekstein v. Severo Sibirsko Gosudar-
stvernnoe Akcionernoe Olschestro Komseverputj & Bank
for Russian Trade, Ltd., [1933] 1 K. B. 47.

1400. ——.]—CALTHORPE'S CASE, No. 1393,
ante.

1401. ——.]—K. was sued in the Exchequer to
answer to the Crown for money received by him
of the abbot of F. to pay over to the abbot of C.
who was attainted of treason. A bill from the
abbot of F. to the abbot of C. was shewn which
was unsealed. On demurrer:—*Held :* the bill
was only a chose in action, there was a contract
nudum pactum, & the action would be dismissed ;
but if a servant received money to the use of his
master, & brought it to the house of the master,
who was afterwards attainted, this would be
forfeit.—H. v. KITCHEN (1582), Sav. 40 ; 123
E. R. 1000.

1402. ——.]—On application being made to a
widow for payment for goods supplied to her late
husband, she promised, in consideration of the
creditor supplying her, to pay the amount due
from her late husband & the price of goods to be
supplied to her by a certain day:—*Held :* the
action would lie, & there was a good consideration ;
for the forbearance of the money was a good consideration in itself, & in every *assumpsit*, he who
made the promise ought to have benefit thereby,
& the other was to sustain some loss.—HATCH &
CAPEL'S CASE (1613), Godb. 202 ; 78 E. R. 123.

Illustration V: ENGLISH AND EMPIRE DIGEST

Vol. 12—Contract. Cases 483—3218: *400a—*1733a

87

Part V.—Consideration

1397. **Refd.** D. P. P. v. Turner, [1973] 3 All E. R. 124.

1411. **Refd.** *Re* Wyvern Developments, Ltd., [1974] 2 All E. R. 535.

1484. **Distd.** Harris Simon & Co., Ltd. v. Manchester City Council, [1975] 1 All E. R. 412.

*919a. *Agreement to pay higher price.*]—GILBERT STEEL, LTD. v. UNIVERSITY CONSTRUCTION, LTD. (1973).—CAN. *See* Continuation Vol. D.

*920. **Add. Citations** (*after* 9 D. L. R. (3d) 425):—*on appeal sub nom.* TANENBAUM v. SEARS, [1972] S. C. R. 67.

*945a. *Promise to perform household services.*]—SWAN v. PUBLIC TRUSTEE (1972).—CAN. *See* Continuation Vol. D.

1577. **Folld.** Harrop v. Thompson, [1975] 2 All E. R. 94.

1768. **Refd.** Wachtel v. Wachtel, [1973] 1 All E. R. 829.

*1051a. *Delivery taken of substantial part of goods.*]—ANWAR v. KENYA BEARING CO. (1973).—E. AF. *See* Continuation Vol. D.

2035. **Refd.** The Albazero, [1976] 3 All E. R. 129.

Part VI.—Void and Illegal Contracts

2089. **Refd.** Ashmore, Benson, Pease & Co., Ltd. v. A. V. Dawson, Ltd., [1973] 2 All E. R. 856.

2100. **Refd.** R. v. Southampton JJ., *Ex p.* Green, [1975] 2 All E. R. 1073.

2628. **Distd.** Newman v. Dorrington Developments, Ltd., [1975] 3 All E. R. 928. **Refd.** Ailion v. Spiekermann, [1976] 1 All E. R. 497.

Part VII.—Performance and Excuses for Non-Performance

2733. **Refd.** Potters v. Loppert, [1973] 1 All E. R. 658.

2742. **Apld.** Brown & Davis, Ltd. v. Galbraith, [1972] 3 All E. R. 31.

*1426a. *Sale of land—Whether unilateral right to make time of essence of the contract.*]—BOW v. McGRATH BUILDERS, LTD. (1974).—N.Z. *See* Continuation Vol. D.

2765. **Consd.** Luck v. White (1973), 26 P. & C. R. 89.

2769. **Refd.** United Scientific Holdings, Ltd. v. Burnley Corpn. [1976] 2 All E. R. 220.

2802. (p. 386). *For* Case No. 2732. *read* 2802.

*1469a. *Lease of apartment—Apartment not ready by stated date—Whether waiver of time limit.*]—GLENMORE GARDEN APT., LTD. v. TODD (1972).—CAN. *See* Continuation Vol. D.

2844. **Refd.** Mardorf Peach & Co., Ltd. v. Attica Sea Carriers Corpn. of Liberia, The Laconia, [1976] 2 All E. R. 249.

3032. **Refd.** Chappell v. Times Newspapers, Ltd. [1975] 2 All E. R. 233.

3038. **Refd.** Rother Iron Works, Ltd. v. Canterbury Pre-

ILLUSTRATION VI: ENGLISH AND EMPIRE DIGEST: CUMULATIVE SUPPLEMENT: NOTER-UP

The entry in the *Noter-Up* reads as follows:

Volume 12   CONTRACT
   Part V   Consideration
   1397 Refd. D.P.P. *v.* Turner, [1973] 3 All E.R. 124
   945a Promise to perform household services. — SWAN *v.* PUBLIC
      TRUSTEE (1972) — CAN. *See* Continuation Vol. D

This means that case number 1397 in Volume 12 (which deals
with consideration in contracts) has subsequently been referred to
in *D.P.P.* v. *Turner*. A new topic — promises to perform
household services as a form of consideration — has been inserted
at an appropriate point in the subject sequence. The relevant case is
a Canadian one (CAN.), and full details of the case can be found by
looking up the name of the case (*Swan* v. *Public Trustee*) in the list
of cases at the front of *Continuation Volume D*, where we are told
that a summary of the case and a citation for it will be found on
page 120 of Volume D.

If the entry says "see Division 2, *post*," *e.g.*

ESTOPPEL
   411a General rule] – DOERING v. TOWN OF GRANDVIEW
   (1974) — CAN. *See* Division 2, *post*

this is a reference to the back part of the *Cumulative Supplement*,
where the case will be found summarised under the heading
Estoppel, at case number *411a.

Suppose we want to trace the cases on election law. When we
consult the Index (Vols. 55 to 56) we find that this is dealt with in
Volume 20, which still has a blue band. We can therefore trace the
information in Volume 20 immediately, from the information
provided in the index. Make a note of the volume, the headings
used, and the case numbers. Now look in the *Cumulative Supplement*
under the same heading. This will provide you with a note of any
new cases since the main work was published, and will refer you to
the appropriate *Continuation Volume*, or to the back of the
Cumulative Supplement itself, where you will find a summary of the
case, under the appropriate subject heading.

SUMMARY: USING THE ENGLISH AND EMPIRE DIGEST TO FIND CASES ON A SUBJECT

(1) Look up the subject in the Consolidated Index (Vols. 55 to 56) and note the volume number (in bold type), page number and case number (in italics).

(2) If the volume referred to has a blue band, turn to the appropriate page and locate the correct case number.

(3) If the volume referred to has a green band, use the Reference Adaptor to convert the case number given in the index to the new case number.

(4) To bring the information up to date, consult the Cumulative Supplement under the appropriate subject heading. This will provide you with any new cases since the main work was published and will also give you the subsequent judicial history of any case referred to in the main volume. Where the reference is to a new case, you will be referred to an entry in the Continuation Volumes or in the back of the Cumulative Supplement itself, where you will find the case summarised.

PROBLEMS

(a) In which volumes do the following subjects appear?
Education
Mortgage

(b) Give the volume, page and case numbers where you can find cases dealing with the obligations of a solicitor towards his client.

6-13. *How to Use Individual Indexes to Series of Law Reports to Trace Cases on a Subject*

If the facilities in your library are limited, you may need to use the indexes to individual series of law reports to trace relevant cases on a subject. The most useful are the **Law Reports Indexes** (para. 2-16) because they cover a number of other important series in

HOW TO TRACE CASES ON A SUBJECT
IN THE ENGLISH AND EMPIRE DIGEST

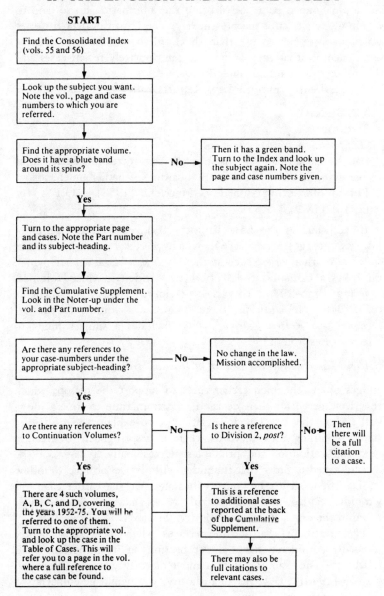

START

Find the Consolidated Index (vols. 55 and 56)

Look up the subject you want. Note the vol., page and case numbers to which you are referred.

Find the appropriate volume. Does it have a blue band around its spine? —**No**→ Then it has a green band. Turn to the Index and look up the subject again. Note the page and case numbers given.

Yes

Turn to the appropriate page and cases. Note the Part number and its subject-heading.

Find the Cumulative Supplement. Look in the Noter-up under the vol. and Part number.

Are there any references to your case-numbers under the appropriate subject-heading? —**No**→ No change in the law. Mission accomplished.

Yes

Are there any references to Continuation Volumes? —**No**→ Is there a reference to Division 2, *post*? —**No**→ Then there will be a full citation to a case.

Yes　　　　　　　　　　　**Yes**

There are 4 such volumes, A, B, C, and D, covering the years 1952-75. You will be referred to one of them. Turn to the appropriate vol. and look up the case in the Table of Cases. This will refer you to a page in the vol. where a full reference to the case can be found.

This is a reference to additional cases reported at the back of the Cumulative Supplement.

There may also be full citations to relevant cases.

addition to the *Law Reports*. Indexes are available covering 1951–1960, 1961–1970 and supplementary indexes (a red index and a pink index: para. 2-16) bring the information up to date to within a few weeks of the present day. The **Law Reports Indexes** are probably easier to use than the **English and Empire Digest** but remember that they only cover comparatively recent cases and that foreign cases are not included.

A typical entry from the **Law Reports Index** is given below:

TRIBUNAL
Statutory
"Independent person" as chairman
Barrister chairman of disciplinary committee of agricultural marketing board — Paid fee by board — Whether independent. **Potato Marketing Board v. Merricks** [1958] 2 Q.B. 316; [1958] 3 W.L.R. 135

In addition to the **Law Reports Indexes** (and the series of Digests, going back to 1865, which preceded them), there are indexes to other series, such as the *All England Law Reports*, which publishes a **Consolidated Tables and Index** in three volumes, covering 1936–1976. This is kept up to date by supplements (para. 2-16). In addition, there is an index volume to the *All England Law Reports Reprint*, which includes a subject index to selected cases from 1558–1935.

6.14.   *How to Trace the Subsequent Judicial History of a Case*

Judges often rely upon earlier cases to support the reasons which they have given for their decision, and from time to time a judge will review the case law in an attempt to explain the principles stated in earlier cases, or to use them as a springboard to create a new application of the principles. Occasionally a case will be distinguished in order that the judge will not feel obliged to follow it. Less frequently, the court will state that the earlier case was wrongly decided, and will overrule it, so that the principles laid down in the case will not be followed thereafter.

The treatment that a case receives when it is subsequently judicially considered has a direct bearing on its importance and reliability. For example, if in a moot or essay you cited *Keppel* v. *Douglas* [1946] Ch. 42, as an authority, you would be embarrassed to discover that it was overruled by statute; similarly, you should be aware that the case of *The Albazero* [1975] 3 W.L.R. 491 was reversed on appeal to the House of Lords. Consequently you must be alert to the need to trace the subsequent judicial history of a particular case.

The simplest way to do this is to use the **Current Law Case Citator** and the **Current Law Citator** (para. 2-14). These will give the citation to any English case which has been judicially considered since 1947 and show its treatment. For instance, the well-known old case *Carlill* v. *Carbolic Smoke Ball Co.*, which was reported in 1892, appears in the *Current Law Case Citator* because it has been considered in court several times since 1947. After giving the name of the case, and a reference to where the case is to be found in the *Law Reports*, the following entry appears:

Dicta applied, 67/1745: *Applied*, 73/1529: *Distinguished*, 73/3095

This means that if you turn to the *Current Law Year Book* for 1967, item 1745 will be found to be the summary of a case in which *Carlill's* case was applied. Similarly, the 1973 *Year Book* contains two reports of cases (items 1529 and 3095) in which the case was considered.

The **Law Reports Indexes** contain a heading "Cases judicially considered," and the **Index to the All England Law Reports** also includes a list of "Cases reported and considered." The **English and Empire Digest** (para. 2-15) contains annotations to entries, showing the subsequent judicial history of a case. This is kept up to date by the information in the *Noter-up* part of the *Cumulative Supplement*.

6-15. HOW TO FIND WORDS AND PHRASES
JUDICIALLY CONSIDERED

The meaning of words is of great importance to lawyers. The interpretation of statutes and documents may hinge upon the meaning of a single word. For example, does "day" in banking terms mean 24 hours, or does it end at the close of working hours? Can a mistress be considered part of a "family"?

A number of specialised dictionaries record the courts' decisions on problems such as these. **Stroud's Judicial Dictionary**, in five volumes, provides the meaning of words as defined in the case law and in statutes. **Words and Phrases Legally Defined** is a similar publication, which is kept up to date by supplements.

The **Law Reports Indexes** include a heading "Words and phrases" in which full details of cases defining a particular word or phrase are given.

> *e.g.* "Gain" — Theft Act 1968, s. 17. **Reg.** v. **Eden**, C.A. (1971) 55 Cr. App.R. 193

Current Law, and the **Current Law Year Books**, also include an entry "Words and phrases," and the **Indexes** to the **All England Law Reports** have a similar entry.

6-16.   HOW TO TRACE STATUTES ON A SUBJECT

6-17.   *Statutes in Force*

Statutes in Force contains the Public General Acts at present in force in the United Kingdom. This looseleaf edition, published by HMSO, commenced in 1972, and it is still being issued. The work is arranged alphabetically by subject, and each subject has its own index. This provides the relevent details of year, chapter number, and section number to enable you to trace the legislation dealing with a particular aspect of a topic. Currently you must "guess" the subject heading which will cover the area of your interest. However there are both alphabetical and chronological lists of all Acts published in the series, giving the subject headings under which they appear. When the work is complete there will be a general index. An annual Cumulative Supplement is published for each subject covered, bringing the information on that topic up to date. Remember that the edition is incomplete and it may not contain the information you seek.

PROBLEMS

In what subject group will the following Acts be found:
Wills Act 1968
Law of Property Act 1925

6-18.   *Index to the Statutes*

A detailed alphabetical index to the statute law on a particular
subject will be found in the **Index to the Statutes**. This is
unfortunately several years behind in publication, so it will be
necessary to consult **Halsbury's Statutes** (para. 6-19) or the
Current Law Statute Citator (para. 6-25) to ensure that there
have not been any recent changes.

   The **Index to the Statutes** is comprehensive. It gives a
complete list of all the statutes dealing with a particular subject
which are still in force, and then provides a detailed analysis of
each subject, showing the section and subsections of all statutes
which are relevant to that topic. Cross-references are given from
one entry to another. A typical entry is reproduced below:

SEVERN
   1965 c. 24 Severn Bridge Tolls
   Navigation weirs, provision as to, *See* FISHERIES, 3
   Severn Bridge –
      tolls: 1965 c. 24, ss. 1-5, schs. 1, 2
      obstruction and damage, prevention of: 1965 c. 24 ss. 7-9
      ferries: extinguishment and compensation: 1965 c. 24 ss.
      10-11

   Where the law relating to England and Scotland is different, the
relevant law is prefaced by E. (England) or S. (Scotland). Under
some subject headings the topics are subdivided according to area,
where the law relating to different regions differs. For instance, the
law relating to agricultural holdings in England and Scotland is
different, and there are therefore two main subject headings:
Agricultural holdings, England, and Agricultural holdings, Scotland.

6-19.   *Halsbury's Statutes of England*

The series of **Halsbury's Statutes of England**, which is now in its
third edition, is arranged alphabetically by subject. The purpose of
the series is to provide the correct and amended text of legislation,
of whatever date, which is still in force. It includes all Public
General Acts in force in England and Wales, although a few Acts
of limited importance have been omitted. The text of each Act is

accompanied by Notes which provide, for example, judicial interpretation of relevant words and phrases, relevant statutory instruments made under the Act, case law, cross references to other sections, and references to relevant sections of **Halsbury's Laws of England**.

The main work is issued in 39 volumes. Since 1968, *Continuation Volumes* have been issued, usually on an annual basis. These contain the texts of Acts passed during a particular year, arranged under the same subject headings as are used in the main work. A *Cumulative Supplement* brings the information in the main work and the *Continuation Volumes* up to date, and a looseleaf *Noter-Up Volume* states the most recent changes. A companion volume, entitled *Current Statutes Service*, contains the annotated text of Acts published during the current year. These are later replaced by annual *Continuation Volumes*.

6-20.   HOW TO USE HALSBURY'S STATUTES TO TRACE
                  INFORMATION ON A SUBJECT

1. Consult the *Table of Statutes and Index* (which covers Volumes 1-45). This will guide you to the relevant entries in both the main work and in the *Continuation Volumes* 40 to 45. Entries give the volume number in **bold** type, and the page number, *e.g.*

BACK-TO-BACK HOUSES
   prohibition on erection of, 16, 118

2. When you have found the relevant entries, note the subject heading under which they appear, and the page numbers.

3. Check in the *Cumulative Supplement*, under the subject heading which you have consulted in the main work, and you will find there details of any alterations or amendments to both the main work and the *Continuation Volume* entries for that subject. At the beginning of each subject heading there is a list of all Acts passed on that subject since the main volume was published indicating, for each one, where it is to be found in the *Continuation Volumes*.

4. Finally, check in the looseleaf *Noter-Up* Volume, under the same subject heading, for any very recent changes. This will refer you to the *Current Statutes Service* volume if there has been any legislation on that subject during the current year.

6-21.   HOW TO TRACE A SPECIFIC STATUTE IN HALSBURY'S
STATUTES

1. Check the *Table of Statutes and Index* to Volumes 1 to 45. At
the front of the index there are alphabetical and chronological lists
of all Acts which were still in force in January 1976, showing the
subject heading(s) under which each Act is printed, and the
relevant volume and page. Note that some Acts are printed under
more than one subject heading. For instance, part of the
Agriculture Act 1937 appears under three different headings:
Agriculture, Land Drainage and Animals.

2. If the entry in the index is printed in *italic* type this indicates
that this Act has been repealed and is no longer law.

3. If the Act you want has been issued since the end of 1975,
look in the list of statutes which appears at the front of the
Cumulative Supplement. This again will indicate the volume and
page in the *Continuation Volumes* where you will find the text
printed in full.

4. The text of any Act passed during the last year or eighteen
months will be found in the looseleaf *Current Statutes Service*
volume.

SUMMARY

To trace Acts on a subject:
(1)   consult index to Volumes 1 to 45
(2)   consult relevant entries and note subject headings used
(3)   consult same subject headings in *Cumulative Supplement*. A
list of Acts printed in the *Continuation volumes* is printed at
the beginning of each subject heading
(4)   consult *Noter-Up Current Service* volume, under appropriate
subject heading.
To trace a particular Act:
(1)   if passed before 1976 consult alphabetical or chronological
lists in index to Volumes 1 to 45
(2)   if passed after 1976, consult list at front of *Cumulative
Supplement*
(3)   if passed during current year, look in the looseleaf *Current
Statutes Service* volume.

PROBLEMS

(a)   What legislation covers rabies?

(b)   S.I. 1974 No. 2211 applied to section 3 of the above legislation. Has the S.I. been amended?

(c)   What Act in 1977 amended the above legislation?

HOW TO TRACE STATUTES ON A SUBJECT, USING HALSBURY'S STATUTES

START

Find the Table of Statutes and Index for volumes 1-45. Look up the topic you require in the Index. Have you found it?

— No → Consult the Indexes to Halsbury's Laws. This should enable you to trace relevant information.

Yes

Note the volume and page. Find the appropriate volume and note the subject heading under which the information is entered.

Find the Cumulative Supplement.

Is there an entry in the Cumulative Supplement under that subject heading for the volume and page which you have consulted?

— Yes → There have been changes since the main and continuation volumes were published. The Cumulative Supplement will give references to the relevant authorities and to continuation volumes where the full text of relevant Acts will be found.

No

Find the Current Statutes Service Noter-up.

Turn to the appropriate continuation volumes and look up the subject heading in the index at the back of the volumes.

Is there an entry for the volume and page number under the subject heading you have been consulting?

— Yes → There have been some recent changes in the law. The Noter-up will give references to the relevant authorities.

No

You are now up to date.

If there is a reference to a recent statute, this is printed in the Current Statutes Service.

HOW TO LOCATE A SPECIFIC STATUTE IN HALSBURY'S STATUTES, IF YOU KNOW THE SHORT TITLE OF THE ACT

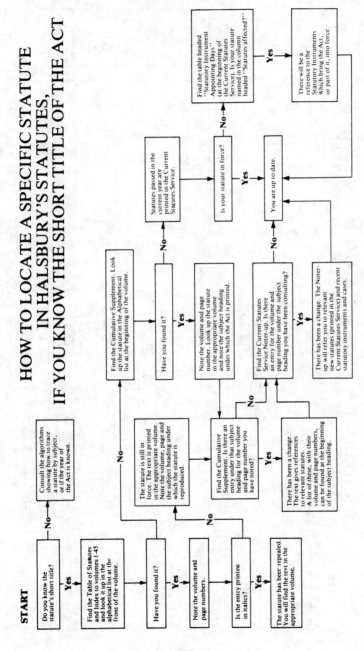

START

Do you know the statute's short title? — **No** → Consult the algorithms showing how to trace a statute by subject, or if the year of the Act is known.

Yes ↓

Find the Table of Statutes and Index to volumes 1-45 and look it up in the alphabetical list at the front of the volume.

↓

Have you found it? — **No** → The statute is still in force. The text is printed in the appropriate volume. Note the volume, page and the subject heading under which the statute is reproduced.

Yes ↓

Note the volume and page numbers.

↓

Is the entry printed in italics? — **No** → Find the Cumulative Supplement. Is there an entry under that subject heading for the volume and page number you have noted?

Yes ↓

The statute has been repealed. You will find the text in the appropriate volume.

Find the Cumulative Supplement. Is there an entry under that subject heading for the volume and page number you have noted? — **No** → (to) Find the Current Statutes Service Noter-up.

Yes ↓

There has been a change. The text gives references to relevant statutes. A list of these, with their volume and page numbers, can be found at the beginning of the subject heading.

Find the Cumulative Supplement. Look up the statute in the Alphabetical list at the beginning of the volume.

↓

Have you found it? — **No** → Statutes passed in the current year are printed in the Current Statutes Service.

Yes ↓

Note the volume and page number. Look up the statute in the appropriate volume and note the subject heading under which the Act is printed.

↓

Find the Current Statutes Service Noter-up. Is there an entry for the volume and page number under the subject heading you have been consulting? — **No** → (connects onward)

Yes ↓

There has been a change. The Noter-up will refer you to relevant new statutes (printed in the Current Statutes Service) and recent statutory instruments and cases.

Statutes passed in the current year are printed in the Current Statutes Service.

↓

Is your statute in force? — **No** → Find the table headed "Statutory Instrument Appointing Days" (at the beginning of the Current Statutes Service). Is your statute named in the column headed "Statutes affected?"

Yes ↓

You are up to date.

Find the table headed "Statutory Instrument Appointing Days" ... Is your statute named in the column headed "Statutes affected?" — **Yes** → There will be a reference to the Statutory Instruments which bring the Act, or part of it, into force.

↓

You are up to date.

HOW TO TRACE A SPECIFIC STATUTE IN HALSBURY'S STATUTES, IF THE YEAR OF THE ACT IS KNOWN

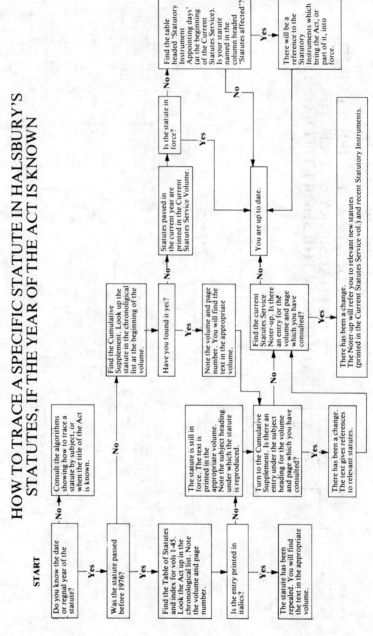

6-22.   *Other Sources for Tracing Legislation on a Subject*

Halsbury's Laws of England (para. 6-3) contains references to relevant statutes, although the text of the Acts is not printed. **Current Law** and the **Current Law Year Book** (paras. 6-9, 6-10) are arranged by subject and include entries for new statutes as well as for cases on a subject. A brief summary of Acts appears under the appropriate subject heading.

The full text of statutes still in force on a particular subject will be found in **Statutes in Force** and **Halsbury's Statutes**. The text of statutes will also be found printed in **Statutes of the Realm** (para. 3-17), **Statutes at Large** (para. 3-18), **Public General Acts** (para. 3-7), **Law Reports: Statutes** (para. 3-10) and **Current Law Statutes** (para. 3-12).

6-23.   CHECKING WHETHER LEGISLATION IS IN FORCE OR HAS BEEN AMENDED

Halsbury's Statutes

The index to Volumes 1 to 45 of **Halsbury's Statutes** serves as a guide to the statute law on a subject which was in force in January 1976. By using the *Cumulative Supplement* and the *Noter-Up* in the *Current Statutes Service* volume (para. 6-21), subsequent amendments or changes can be traced. The *Current Statutes Service* volume contains a list of "Statutory Instruments Appointing Days," showing when a particular Act, or section of an Act, is brought into force by a statutory instrument.

PROBLEM

Has the Children Act 1975, s. 37 been affected by subsequent legislation?

6-24.   *Chronological Table of the Statutes*

The **Chronological Table of the Statutes** is an official publication which lists every statute which has been passed since 1235, and shows, for each one, whether it is still law. This is done by the use of different type faces — an entry in *italic* type indicates that the statute in question is no longer law, whilst entries in **bold** type represent Acts which are still wholly or partly in force. The use of a number of abbreviations can make the entries appear a little confusing.

The entries are arranged in date order. Let us suppose that you wish to discover if any part of the Children and Young Persons Act 1956 is still law. Turn to the entries for 1956, and locate the relevant entry (4 & 5 Eliz. 2, c. 24). The entry, which is reproduced below, is printed in *italic* type. This is an indication that the Act is *not* in force:

1956 (4 & 5 Eliz. 2)
      c. 24. *Children and Young Persons*. — **r.** (S.), Social Work (S.), 1968 (c. 49), s. 95(2), sch. 9 pt. I; (E.), Children and Young Persons, 1969 (c. 54), s. 72(4), sch. 6.

This tells us that the statute was repealed (r.) in respect of Scotland (S.) by the Social Work (Scotland) Act 1968 (c. 49), s. 95(2) and Schedule 9, Part I; and in England (E.) the Act was repealed by the Children and Young Persons Act 1969, s. 72(4).

The adjoining entry (4 & 5 Eliz. 2, c. 23) for the Leeward Islands Act, is printed in **bold** type. This indicates that part of this Act is still law, although the entry tells you that sections 1, 3, 4 and 5 and the Schedule were repealed by the West Indies Act 1962, s. 10(3). A list of the abbreviations used will be found at the front of the volume.

PROBLEM

Is the Colonial Stock Act 1934, c. 47 in force?

Unfortunately, the **Chronological Table** is usually about two years out of date. To check whether there has been a more recent change in the law it will be necessary to check in the annual publication entitled **The Public General Acts and General Synod Measures: 19 . Tables and Index,** in the section entitled "Effect of legislation." This shows whether the Acts passed during that year have amended or repealed any previous legislation. Like the **Chronological Table,** the entries in this index are arranged by the date of the original Act, so that it is possible to tell at a glance if there has been any change to a particular statute. The *Public General Acts: Table and Index* is published separately by HMSO and it is also printed at the end of the annual volumes of the *Public General Acts and Measures*. Alternatively, you can use the **Current Law Statute Citator** to bring the information in the **Chronological Table** up to date.

6-25.   *Current Law Statute Citator*

The **Current Law Statute Citator** enables you to check whether any statute has been repealed or amended by legislation since 1947 and also to trace cases on the interpretation of a statute since that date. A bound volume covers the period 1947–1971. The period from 1972 to the end of last year is covered in the **Current Law Statute Citator.** (If your library has the Scottish edition of *Current Law* this is called the **Scottish Current Law Citator.** Despite the name, it includes all English statutes.)

Changes made during the current year are given in a supplementary **Current Law Statute Citator and Index** which is issued three times a year as part of the **Current Law Statutes** series. Changes too recent to be included in the latest supplement can be found by looking under the appropriate heading in the monthly issues of *Current Law.*

Entries in the **Citators** are arranged by date, and cover Acts passed since the thirteenth century, showing, for each one, whether there have been any alterations or amendments to the text, or whether the Act has been repealed since 1947. Any statutory instruments made under a particular Act are also shown, together with any cases on the construction of the statute, and information on where these are to be found. A typical entry is reproduced below:

1967
CAP.
1. **Land Commission Act 1967**
   s. 11, repealed in pt.: 1975, c. 76, sch. 2.
   ss. 15, 58, 89, 99, schs. 15, 16 amended: 1972, c. 52, sch. 21
   s. 51, order 74/974.
   s. 99, see *Alexandra Transport Co.* v. *Secretary of State for Scotland*,
        1974 S.L.T. 81.

This indicates that part of the Land Commission Act has been repealed, and gives you the citation of the repealing statute, together with details of the statute which amended certain sections of the Act. A statutory instrument (order), number S.I. 1974/974 was made under the provisions of section 51 of the Act. The full details of the instrument will be found in the annual volumes of statutory instruments. Also in 1974 there was a case — *Alexandra Transport Co.* v. *Secretary of State for Scotland* — which turned on the interpretation of section 99 of the Act. This will be found reported in the 1974 volume of the *Scots Law Times* (S.L.T.) at page 81.

PROBLEMS

(a)   Within the last few years chapter 15 of the Statute of Westminster II, 1285 (13 Edw. 1) has been repealed. Give the citation of the repealing Act.

(b)   Give the names of recent cases, after 1972, which have turned on the interpretation of section 1 of the Theft Act 1968.

Very recent changes in the law can be traced in **Current Law**, or by consulting the weekly practitioners' journals, such as the **New Law Journal** and **Solicitors' Journal**.

6-26.   HOW TO TRACE STATUTORY INSTRUMENTS
ON A SUBJECT

6-27.   *Halsbury's Statutory Instruments*

Halsbury's Statutory Instruments is a series which covers every statutory instrument of general application and in force in England and Wales. It reproduces the text of a selected number and provides summaries of a number of others. The series is arranged by subject matter. There are two independent methods of using it to find an instrument. When the year and number (or date if unnumbered) is known use the *Chronological List of Instruments* which is found in the Service Binder. If these details are not known use the *General Index* which classifies instruments according to subject matter. Consult the updating *Cumulative Supplementary Index* at the back of the *General Index*, Volume 24. When using the series remember to check the *Annual Cumulative Supplement* and the *Quarterly Survey* (both of which are in the looseleaf *Service* Volume) which constitute the updating service.

PROBLEMS

(a) What Statutory instrument covers "air navigation, restrictions on flying over atomic energy establishments"?

(b) Which establishments are covered by this S.I.?

(c) Give the title of the following S.I.'s:
S.R. & O. 1929, No. 534
S.I. 1952, No. 2232

6.28 *Index to Government Orders*

The **Index to Government Orders** is arranged alphabetically by subject and enables you to trace statutory instruments which were in force at the time the **Index** was issued, and which deal with a particular subject. Where there are a large number of entries under a particular subject heading, the subject is divided into a number of subsections. For instance, under the heading "Community Land" there are a number of sub-headings, — "Acquisition and appropriation of land," "Planning permission," "Land compensation," etc.

Every entry gives the statute under which a power to make statutory instruments was conferred, and the instruments which have been made under the provisions of that statute. If the power conferred by the Act has not yet been exercised (*i.e.* if no statutory instruments have been made under a particular Act) this is stated. Suppose, for instance, that you were interested in locating the law relating to the use of poisons for killing animals regarded as pests. Under the heading "Animals" there are a large number of entries, which have been subdivided. A relevant entry is found under "Animals — prevention of cruelty" in the sub-section "Use of poisons."

ANIMALS
1. **Prevention of cruelty**
   (5) USE OF POISONS
   Power
   1962 Secretary of State, if satisfied that a poison cannot be used for

destroying animals without causing undue suffering, and that
other, adequate, methods of destroying them exist, may by regs.
made by S.I. prohibit or restrict use of that poison for destroying
animals, or animals of any description.
   S.I. to be subject to annulment on resolution of either House.
   Animals (Cruel Poisons) Act 1962 (c. 26) s. 2
Exercise
1963/1278 Animals (Cruel Poisons) Regs. . . . 1963 II,
p. 2131.

This indicates that the powers conferred under section 2 of the
Animals (Cruel Poisons) Act 1962 were exercised by Statutory
Instrument number 1278, passed in 1963. This is to be found in the 1963
volumes of **Statutory Instruments**, in the second (II) part, at page
2131.

PROBLEMS

(a)   Under the heading "Bee diseases" there will be found an entry relating
to the Foul Brood Disease of Bees Order. Give the year and number of
this instrument.

(b)   Under the same heading (Bee Diseases) there appears the Importation
of Bees Order. What statute was this Order made under?

6-29.   *Tracing Recent Statutory Instruments and Amendments*

Statutory instruments on a subject which have been passed since
the latest **Index to Government Orders** was published may be
traced by consulting the indexes to the bound volumes of *Statutory
Instruments*, and, for more recent changes, the monthly and annual
Lists of Statutory Instruments, which contain entries in subject
order. If you suspect that there has been a very recent change, it
may be necessary to go through the **Daily List of Government
Publications** (para. 5-14) for the past few weeks, which will bring
the information in the latest monthly *List* up to date. However,
students will probably seldom need to go to these lengths. Recent
instruments can also be traced by looking in **Current Law** or in
the *Monthly Reviews* (filed in the looseleaf *Service* binder) issued with

Halsbury's Laws of England (under the appropriate subject heading) or by using **Halsbury's Statutory Instruments**, where the information is kept up to date by supplements inserted at the back of the volumes. New instruments are also noted weekly in the **Solicitor's Journal** and the **New Law Journal**.

If you suspect that the text of an instrument has been changed or amended, *Halsbury's Statutory Instruments*, or one of the specialist looseleaf encyclopedias (if there is one available covering your subject field), is probably the easiest place to trace the up-dated version of the instrument. Amendments to the text can be traced in the **Table of Government Orders** (para. 6-31).

6-30. *Tracing Statutory Instruments made under a Particular Act*

If you know the name of an Act, and you wish to find out if any statutory instrument has been made under that Act, you should consult the *Table of Statutes* which appears at the front of the **Index to Government Orders**. This will indicate under which subject heading(s) entries relating to that Act appear in the Index. For instance, suppose you wish to trace what instruments were made under the powers conferred by the Metropolitan Police Act 1839, s. 52. If you look in the *Table of Statutes* at the front of the volume, this informs you that the powers conferred under this Act are dealt with under the heading "Police," section 7. The relevant entry in the *Table of Statutes*, and in the main work, are reproduced below (with minor omissions for the sake of greater clarity):

Table of Statutes
1839 (2-3 V.)
    c. 47 **Metropolitan Police**
        s. 52 . . . POLICE, 7
Index
POLICE
    7 Traffic Wardens
Power
1967. O. may provide that for purposes of functions which traffic wardens authorised to discharge, reference to constable, etc. in following enactments to include traffic warden:-
Metropolitan Police Act 1839 (c. 47) s. 52;

[Transport Act 1968 (c. 73), s. 131(6); Road Traffic Act 1972 (c. 20), sched. 7]
Exercise
1970/1958 Functions of Traffic Wardens O. 1970 III, p. 6409

The information can be brought up to date by consulting the latest issue of the **Current Law Citator** (*Statute Citator*) (para. 6-25).

6-31.   *Finding out if a Statutory Instrument is still in Force*

If you know the number of a Statutory Instrument you can check whether it is still in force by consulting the **Table of Government Orders**. This is a list, in date order, of all instruments passed since 1671, and it shows, for each one, whether it was still in force when the volume was published. If the entry is in **bold** type then it is wholly or partly in force; if it appears in *italics* then the instrument is no longer law. Entries in **bold** type indicate whether any changes have been made in the instrument since 1948 (the text as it stood in December 1948 will be found in **Statutory Rules and Orders and Statutory Instruments Revised**). Full details of the abbreviations used will be found in the Introduction to the volumes. The Table is produced annually, and the information is brought up to date between editions by a Noter-Up. Part of a typical entry is reproduced below:

    1971
        414 **Probation (Allowances) Rules**
            rule 5 replaced, 1976/116
            am[ended]., 1976/2119
            sch. 1 replaced, 1972/1400
            para. 3 am., 1975/592, 1976/2119

6-32.   FINDING BOOKS ON A SUBJECT

Your first task should be to find out what suitable books are available in your own library. We have already explained that the classification scheme (para 1-3) is intended to bring together on the shelves, books dealing with the same subject. You need to consult the **subject index** to find out what classification number has been given to books on your topic. This is an alphabetical list of subjects giving the classification number which has been assigned to each one. If you cannot find the desired subject try some alternative headings, or look under a more general, or a more specific subject. For instance, suppose that you require information on the legal aspects of stopping a life support machine which is keeping a comatosed person alive. You are unlikely to find an entry under life support machine and you may need to look under a number of possible subject headings — euthanasia or mercy-killing, medicine, medical ethics, etc., — in order to find relevant material. Remember that if your topic is not exclusively legal, there may be books on the subject in other parts of the library. You should therefore consult the main library catalogues as well as any catalogues in the law library. If you have any difficulty in finding relevant entries in the subject index ask the library staff for help.

Once you have found the classification number or numbers, you can go to the shelves at that number to see what is available. However, this means that you will inevitably miss some relevant material which is not on the shelves. You should therefore look in the **subject catalogue** under the classification number. There you will find a record for every book which the library possesses on that subject. Remember that more general books may also contain a chapter or substantial sections on your topic.

Footnotes and bibliographies (lists of books) in textbooks and periodical articles will refer to other books, journals and cases on the subject. You can check in the library catalogue to find out if these are available in your library. Remember that government reports on the subject may not be entered in the subject catalogue. You may need to consult the separate indexes to government publications (para. 5-14) to trace these in the library.

To find out what books have been published on a subject, both in this country and abroad, you need to consult **bibliographies**. A number of possible sources of information are given below. Not all of them may be available in your library, and you will probably only need to use one or two of them in order to trace relevant books. You will also see details of how to find out whether a book is still in print (that is, whether it can easily be obtained from a bookseller), and the approximate cost.

6-33.   *Legal Bibliographies*

6-34.   LAW BOOKS PUBLISHED

Law Books Published is issued in several parts during the
year, and these parts are then replaced by an annual volume, giving
details of all books on law and allied topics published during a
particular year. It covers British and American books and some
foreign books written in English. There are entries under authors
and under titles, in a single alphabet. The second half of each
volume is a list of books published on particular subjects during
the year. The subject headings are American as is the spelling, *e.g.*
railroads, labor. The entries under subject headings are not always
consistent. For instance, Erskine May's *Parliamentary Practice* (19th
ed.), appears under the headings "Legislation — Great Britain"
and "Great Britain — Parliament," but not under "Parliamentary
procedure," although another book entitled *Parliamentary Practice*,
by H. M. Robert, is entered under this heading.

PROBLEMS

(a)   Consult the 1976 volume to find a book written by Geoffrey
      Wilson which contains a collection of cases and materials — on
      what subject are these cases?

(b)   Give the author and title of a book written in 1976 on the
      Ombudsman in New Zealand.

6-35.   LAW BOOKS IN PRINT

Law Books in Print is published at intervals, and gives a list of
all the law books which are still in print at the time of publication.
Entries are arranged in the same way as in the companion **Law
Books Published** (*i.e.* under authors, titles and subjects).

6-36.   CURRENT LAW

At the back of each monthly issue of **Current Law** is a list of new books published during that month (mainly British, with a few foreign works in English). Unfortunately, the publishers are not given, although the price is stated. When the monthly issues of **Current Law** are replaced by the **Current Law Year Book**, a list of books published during the year is printed at the back of the *Year Book*, arranged in subject order.

6-37. CURRENT PUBLICATIONS IN LEGAL AND RELATED FIELDS

Current Publications in Legal and Related Fields is published monthly and the monthly parts are replaced by annual volumes. There are entries under authors and titles in the monthly parts. In the annual volume, a detailed subject index at the front of the volume guides you to relevant entries in the main (alphabetically arranged) part of the work. Each item has its own individual number.

PROBLEM

Use the 1976 annual volume to trace a collection of case studies on bail in England.

6-38. OTHER SOURCES

A. G. Chloros, *Bibliographical Guide to the Law of the United Kingdom, the Channel Islands and the Isle of Man* (2nd ed.). This is useful for tracing the names of the leading textbooks in each subject area. Although the editions are now, in many cases, out of date, the majority of the information is still relevant. *Where to Look for Your Law* serves a similar function, although the information about editions is now very much out of date. A recent publication which serves the same purpose, and which should be very useful to students wishing to find out easily what books have been published on their topic, is D. Raistrick and J. Rees, *Lawyers' Law Books*.

PROBLEMS

(a) Use *Where to Look for Your Law* or the *Bibliographical guide* to discover the name of one of the leading textbooks on Copyright Law.

(b) Using *Lawyers' Law Books*, give the name of two books or reports which you could consult to find information on 'D' notices.

Two very detailed bibliographies are Sweet and Maxwell's *Legal Bibliography of the British Commonwealth* (especially useful for tracing older British books) and C. Szladits, *Bibliography on Foreign and Comparative Law* (which covers books and articles in English only).

Many more specialist legal bibliographies are also published *e.g.* R. W. M. Dias, *Bibliography of Jurisprudence*; B. A. Hepple, *Bibliography of the Literature on British and Irish Labour Law*; W. J. Chambliss and R. B. Seidman, *Sociology of the Law; A Research Bibliography*. The library staff will help you to trace relevant bibliographies. Remember that most textbooks will also contain a bibliography on their subject.

6-39. *Non-Legal Bibliographies*

If your library does not possess the specialised legal bibliographies or if you are trying to trace information on a non-legal topic, you can use a number of more general bibliographies, which cover law in addition to other topics.

6-40. TRACING RECENTLY PUBLISHED BOOKS

The main source of information for British books which have been published since 1950 is the **British National Bibliography**. This is published weekly. The last issue of each month has a green cover, and this issue contains an index to all the books published that month. Every few months the information is cumulated. At the end of the year an annual volume is produced containing details of all British books published during that year.

The main arrangement is by subject; entries for law books will be found at the numbers 340–349. Following this there is an alphabetical list of all authors and titles of books included in that issue. The last issue of the month (with a green cover) contains an alphabetical list (by authors and titles) of all books published that month, together with a detailed subject index to all books published during the month. Many government publications (including Acts) are included in the **British National Bibliography**.

A typical main subject entry is reproduced below, with explanations:

345.420262 – Theft. Law. *England*[1]
Smith,[2] John Cyril The Law of Theft / [by] J. C. Smith – 3rd ed.[3] – London: Butterworth, 1977.[4] – xxix, 255p[5]/26cm.[6] Previous ed; 1972. – Bibl: p. xxix[7] – Index. – Includes the text of the Theft Act 1968. ISBN[8] 0–406 – 37904–1 : £9.00 ISBN[8] 0–406 – 37905–x : Pbk: £5.75[9] (B77 – 10272)

[1] Classification number and subject.
[2] Author.
[3] Title and edition.
[4] Place published, publisher's name, date published.
[5] Contains 29 introductory pages and 255 pages of text.
[6] Size of book.
[7] Bibliography on page 29.
[8] International Standard Book Number (useful to booksellers when ordering the book).
[9] Price of paperback (£5.75) and hardback (£9).

The entry under the author reads:

Smith, John Cyril. The Law of Theft, 3rd ed.
Butterworth. £9.00 345.420262. (B 77–10272) ISBN 0–404–37904–1.

If we need any further information we must turn to the entry at 345.420262 (reproduced above).

The title entry is similar:

Law of Theft. (Smith, John Cyril) 3rd ed.
Butterworth. £9.00. 345.420262. (B 77–10272) ISBN 0–406–37904–1.

Finally if we look in the detailed Subject index, (at the back of the volume) the entry reads:

Theft. England
   Law   345.420262.

Thus in every case, for full details we must consult the main subject entry at 345.420262.

PROBLEMS

(a) Using the 1975 annual volume, consult the subject index at the back of the volume. Give the classification number for books on the jurisdiction of justices of the peace in England.

(b) Look up that number in the main subject sequence at the front of the volume. There were two books on justices of the peace published in 1975. Name the authors of both.

(c) Who is the publisher of the first of these two books?
   How much did the book cost?

(d) Use the 1974 annual volume to discover the name of the author of a book entitled *Legal Values in Western Society*.
   Who published this book?

(e) In 1974 the organisation called "Justice" published a report. The title had something to do with roads – find the correct title. Find the full details (author, publisher, date) of a book published in 1974 on the ethics of abortion.

British Books in Print is published annually, and lists all the books published in this country which are still in print. Entries appear under authors and under titles. In some cases the title order is slightly changed, so that the entry appears under the most important words, *e.g.* Law of the Sea, Developments in. Details of the current price, publisher and date are given.

Typical author and title entries are reproduced below:

Bellamy, J. G.[1] Law of Treason in England in the Later Middle Ages[2] D8.[3] xviii, 266.[4] Stud. in English Legal Hist.[5] £8.50. Camb. U.P. (9.70) 521 07830X[6]

[1] Author.
[2] Title.
[3] Code for size of book.
[4] Number of pages.
[5] Series (Studies in English Legal History).
[6] Price, published by Cambridge University Press in Sept. 1970, Standard book number.

Books in Print is an American publication listing all books published or distributed in the United States which are still in print. There are entries under authors and under titles (in separate volumes). There is also a **Subject Guide to Books in Print**. The entry for the same book, by Bellamy, shows the slight difference in the information given:

> **Bellamy, J. G.** Law of Treason in England in the Later Middle Ages. LC 70–111123[1] (Cambridge Studies in English Legal History) 1970. 21.00[2] (ISBN 0 521 07830 X.) Cambridge U. Pr.

[1] Library of Congress number (of use to libraries and booksellers).
[2] Price (in dollars).

Cumulative Book Index contains entries in one sequence, under authors, subjects and titles. It aims to cover all books published in English throughout the world. Headings use American terminology.

The catalogues of large libraries can provide a very useful list of books on a subject. The University of Cambridge has published the library catalogue of the Squire Law Library, one of the great English legal collections. The American Library of Congress publishes a *National Union Catalog* giving details of American and foreign books, in both author and subject orders. The British Museum has published a *General Catalogue of Printed Books* listing, in author order, all the books in the British Museum. This is kept up to date by supplements, and by the *British National Bibliography*.

6-41. TRACING GOVERNMENT PUBLICATIONS ON A SUBJECT

Government publications have already been dealt with in some detail (Chap. 5). However, it may be useful to summarise again the procedure for tracing government publications on a subject. The monthly and annual indexes to **Government Publications** (para. 5-14) are the chief source of information. The annual catalogues are later replaced by a five-yearly volume. There is a subject index at the back of each volume or issue, referring you to the page(s) where full details of relevant publications can be traced. For older publications the **General Indexes** (para. 5-14) covering the period 1900–1949 and 1950–1959 will be useful. For very recent publications, not covered by the latest monthly list, it will be necessary to look through the copies of the **Daily List** (para. 5-14). It may be possible to trace a reference to more important publications on a subject more easily by examining the latest copies of **Current Law**, or by looking through recent issues of weekly journals.

A series of **Sectional Lists** cover the publications which have been produced by a particular government department, *e.g.* the Home Office, which are still in print. These may serve as a form of subject index. If the library binds up its parliamentary publications into sessional sets (para. 5-2), the indexes to each session may be used, if you have some idea of the date of the material. If your library shelves its non-Parliamentary publications by subject, the library's subject catalogue will enable you to trace relevant publications.

If the library maintains a card index to government publications, you should, of course, consult this.

If you know the name of the chairman of a report, but lack any further details, you should consult A. M. Morgan, *British government publications; an index to chairmen and authors, 1941–1966* or (for earlier reports) S. Richard, *British government publications; an index to chairmen and authors, 1900–1940*. More recent reports can be traced under the names of the chairmen in the monthly, annual and five yearly indexes to *Government Publications*, or in the **Index to Chairmen of Committees**, issued every three months by HMSO.

Chapter 7

COMMUNITY LAW

7-1.   INTRODUCTION

For the law student the impact of the United Kingdom's accession
to the European Communities is not restricted to the creation of a
new option of study, Community Law. For Community Law, in
addition to taking effect alongside the domestic legal systems of
member states as an independent and autonomous legal order,
affects and bears implications for the domestic legal systems
themselves. Its impact on the law student is not therefore confined
to the boundaries of a single course but extends, in varying
degrees, to those branches of the law which are more traditionally
the object of study. At the beginning of a course of legal study that
impact is most clearly seen in courses such as Legal Systems and
Constitutional Law. Facility in the handling of Community legal
materials, therefore, ought not to be approached as an expertise to
be acquired solely within the context of a course on Community
Law but rather as an integral part of the research skills of a law
student.

7-2.   TREATIES AND ANCILLARY INSTRUMENTS

The Communities consist of three separate Communities, the
European Coal and Steel Community, the European Economic
Community and the European Atomic Energy Community, each of
which was established by a separate Treaty which defined the
Community's objectives and provided the means to their attain-
ment through the establishment of institutions with their own
powers. These Treaties, as amended, constitute the essential
starting point in the study of Community Law. They are (1) the
Treaty establishing the European Coal and Steel Community,
Paris, 18 April 1951; (2) the Treaty establishing the European
Economic Community, Rome, 25 March 1957; and (3) the Treaty
establishing the European Atomic Energy Community, Rome, 25
March 1957.

To date (1978) there have been four amending Treaties: (1) the Treaty establishing a Single Council and a Single Commission of the European Communities, Brussels, 8 April 1965 (commonly referred to as the Merger Treaty); (2) the Treaty amending certain Budgetary Provisions of the Treaty . . ., Luxembourg, 22 April 1970 (the First Budgetary Treaty); (3) the Treaty concerning the accession of the Kingdom of Denmark, Ireland, the Kingdom of Norway and the United Kingdom of Great Britain and Northern Ireland to the European Economic Community . . ., Brussels, 22 January 1972 (the Accession Treaty); and (4) the Treaty amending certain financial provisions of the Treaties . . ., Brussels, 22 July 1975 (the Second Budgetary Treaty). Reference must also be made to the "Luxembourg Agreement" on relations between the Council and the Commission and on majority voting procedure which, while not falling within the class of Treaties, is fundamental to an understanding of the development and functioning of the Communities. In addition there are a number of ancillary instruments such as the Convention on Jurisdiction and the Enforcement of Civil and Commercial Judgments which may be treated as akin to the Treaties but which are not of the same status.

There are several sources to which the student may refer for these texts. These include, **European Communities: treaties and related instruments** (HMSO 1972); Sweet and Maxwell's (eds.), **European Community Treaties** (3rd ed., 1977); **Halsbury's Statutes of England** (3rd ed.), Vol 42A (European Continuation Volume 1 1952–72); and Sweet and Maxwell's **Encyclopedia of European Community Law**, Volume B. The last two are annotated and kept up to date by supplements.

7-3. SECONDARY LEGISLATION AND ITS CITATION

It is one of the distinctive features of the Communities that they possess their own law-making powers. That feature is most marked in the EEC Treaty where the task of laying down the measures for the attainment of the Community's objectives is, subject to the principles laid down in the Treaty, left to the institutions. The resultant acts take the form under the EEC Treaty of Regulations, Directives and Decisions and under the ECSC Treaty of Decisions and Recommendations.

The citation of acts is based on the form of the act, its number and the year of its enactment, *e.g.*

Decision (usually abbreviated to Dec) $71^a/66^b$
Directive (usually abbreviated to Dir) $72/230$

In the case of regulations the order is reversed, *e.g.*

Reg $1408^b /71^a$

^{a} the year
^{b} the number of the act

All acts are published in the **Official Journal of the European Communities** (O.J.) which has been published in English since January 1, 1973. In the cases of acts enacted prior to January 1, 1973 the reference is to the **Journal Officiel des Communautés Européennes** (J.O.). Special Editions of the **Official Journal** provide authoritative English texts of pre-accession secondary legislation from 1952–1972. The same texts are published in 42 subject volumes by HMSO as **European Communities, Secondary Legislation 1952–1972**, (1973–4). Since 1968 the **Official Journal** has been published in two parts, **Legislation** (L) and **Information and Notices** (C). References to the **Official Journal** are based on the year, the part number and the page number, *e.g.*

Dec 71/66 E.E.C. J.O. 1971^a, $L28^b/15^c$
Dir 72/230 E.E.C. J.O. 1972^a, $L139^b/28^c$
Reg 1408/71 E.E.C. J.O. 1971^a, $L149^b/2^c$

^{a} the year
^{b} the part number
^{c} the page

Two difficulties face the user of the **Official Journal**. The first is the bulk of the published material, which is compounded by the second difficulty, the lack of an adequate indexing system. The adoption of the practice of asterisking and publishing in bold type acts other than those concerning the day-to-day management of agricultural matters has to a certain extent overcome the first difficulty but the second remains and assumes considerable proportions when, for example, one is faced with the task of determining the authoritative text of a much amended regulation. To overcome this problem several annotated texts are available. These include **Halsbury's Statutes of England** (3rd ed.) Vol. 42A, Sweet and Maxwell's **Encyclopedia of European Community Law** Vol. C, and A. E. Kellerman (ed.), **Guide to EEC Legislation** (1979).

PROBLEMS

(a)   Which act is published at O.J. 1977, L302/1?

(b)   Cite in full the acts which it amends.

7-4.   CASE LAW AND ITS CITATION

The jurisprudence of the European Court constitutes the material, second only to the Treaties, to which law students will most frequently have recourse. The citation of cases heard by the Court differs from the reports of cases before a national court in that in addition to the names of the parties each case is referred to by a number, *e.g.*, Case 6/64 *Costa* v. *ENEL* . . . *viz.* the sixth case of 1964. Writers also often refer to cases by their nicknames, *e.g.* the *Dairy products* case; a reference to Case 90 and 91/63.

Here, as in other areas of Community Law, the multilingual basis of the Communities poses particular problems, the rule being that the only authentic version of a case is that in the procedural language of the case. Since January 1, 1953, the Court has published official English reports of proceedings before it, the **European Court Reports**. They are cited, *e.g.* Case 41/74 *Van Duyn* v. *Home Office* [1974] E.C.R. 1337. The The **European Court Reports** also cover pre-accession cases from 1962 to 1972.

Since 1962, unofficial English translations of proceedings before the European Court, decisions of national courts on questions of Community law and decisions of the Commission on restrictive practices have been published in the **Common Market Law**

Reports (C.M.L.R.), which since 1970 have included the text of the European Court's judgments in the procedural language of the case. Unofficial English translations of judgments of the Court before 1962 are to be found in D. G. Valentine, *Court of Justice of the European Communities* (1965), Vol. 2. Where an official version is required use must be made of a version in one of the other official languages of the Communities, the most commonly cited one of which is the **Recueil de la Jurisprudence de la Cour.** Cases reported in the **Recueil** are cited, *e.g.* Case 6/64 *Costa* v. *ENEL* Rec 1967, 1141.

In addition *The Times* publishes occasional reports of cases heard before the European Court, the **Times European Law Reports.**

PROBLEMS

(a) Which case is to be found at [1974] E.C.R. 631?

(b) Give the *Recueil*, *European Court Report* and *Common Market Law Report* references for Case 13/61 *Bosch* v. *de Geus*

7-5. SECONDARY SOURCES

Where an introduction to a subject is sought a useful start may be made by consulting the index to the **Encyclopedia of European Community Law.** In general, however, the rules which apply to the tracing of materials in other legal subjects apply also in the case of Community law. Reference ought therefore, in addition, to be made to the **Index to Legal Periodicals** and the **Index to Foreign Legal Periodicals.** Two useful introductory bibliographies specifically concerned with Community law are **Community Law: A Selection of Publications on the Law of the European Community and the Relevant Law of the Original Member States** (British and Irish Association of Law Librarians, 1973), and **Where to Find Your Community Law** (British Institute of International and Comparative Law, 1973).

More specialised bibliographies are provided in the **Communities' Documentation Bulletin**. As regards periodicals there was until recently only one legal periodical in English, the **Common Market Law Review** (1963). To this has been added the **European Law Review** (1976) and **Legal Issues of European Integration** (1974). Useful material may also be found in the **Journal of Common Market Studies** (1962). Reference ought also to be made to the other European legal periodicals. These include **Cahiers de Droit Européen** (1965), **Revue du Marché Commun** (1958), **Revue trimestrielle de Droit Européen** (1965), **Europarecht** (1966), and **Rivista di Dirrito Europeo** (1961). In addition much valuable information is contained in the **Bulletin of the European Communities**, its supplements, and the **Annual General Report on the activities of the Communities**.

PROBLEMS

(a) Who wrote "The Powers of the European Community and the Achievement of the Economic and Monetary Union", (1972) *Common Market Law Review* 2?

(b) Who wrote "The Concept of Measures having an Effect Equivalent to Quantitative Restrictions", (1977) *European Law Review* 105?

Chapter 8

PUBLIC INTERNATIONAL LAW

8-1. INTRODUCTION

International law is in many ways quite different from municipal (or national) law. Its methods and materials are often quite distinct from those familiar to the municipal lawyer. The international law collection may, indeed, be housed apart from the rest of the law library, and books on various aspects of international law will commonly be found in collections relating to other subjects such as politics or history. The very question of the use of materials for the derivation of rules of international law is exceedingly complex, and here it is possible to give only a brief description of the most common general international legal materials.

International law has no legislature and no system of binding precedent. Its rules derive their binding force either from inclusion in treaties or conventions, in which case they are binding only upon parties to the treaty, or from their recognition as rules of customary international law. Where states adopt a uniform and consistent practice in a given matter because they regard that practice as being required of them by international law, that practice is said to constitute a rule of customary international law. This customary law is then binding on the whole community of states, with the exception only of those states which have expressly dissented from the rule. Where treaty law and state practice do not supply a direct answer to his problem, the international lawyer has recourse to general principles of law recognised in all, or most, of the legal systems of the world, in order to fill the gaps. In addition, as ever-larger areas of international relations come to be regulated by international organisations, the lawyer may need to examine the practice of relevant organisations in order to determine how they would deal with his problem. This organisational practice may also be of more general interest, in that it may illustrate the attitude of states to certain questions of international law.

These materials will now be described. Much fuller treatment

139

will be found in C. Parry, *Sources and Evidences of International Law* (1965) and in the *Manual of Public International Law* (1968), ed. M. Sorensen, Chap. 3 and pp. 855–892.

8-2.   TREATIES

8-3.   *General Collections*

There are several series of Treaties. The **Consolidated Treaty Series** (1969), ed. C. Parry, covers the period 1648–1880 (although it is intended to extend to 1918–1920) and reproduces the treaties which are found in early collections now out of print. Treaties of all the European powers are included and wherever possible a translation into French or English is given. The treaties are arranged chronologically, and index volumes are due to be published. This Series will cover the period up to the beginning of the **League of Nations Treaty Series** (LNTS) in 1920, which includes treaties concluded, in general, between 1920 and 1939. The **United Nations Treaty Series** (UNTS) covers the period 1946 to the present day. It includes all treaties and international agreements registered or filed and recorded with the United Nations.

8-4.   *Other Collections*

There are a number of collections of treaties selected according to various criteria. Most important are the official national treaty collections. The **United Kingdom Treaty Series** (UKTS) runs from 1892–date, while British treaties too early to fall within the *Consolidated Treaty Series* appear in **Rymer's Foedera** (20 vols., 1704–1735), covering the period 1101–1625. The series of **British and Foreign State Papers** contains a selection of British and Foreign treaties from the early nineteenth century onwards. Several other states produce national treaty series, notably the **United States Treaty Series**, and some international organisations, such as the Council of Europe, also publish their own treaty collections. There are further unofficial collections selected by subject, for example, A. J. Peaslee's **International Governmental Organizations** (4 vols., 1974–76) and **New Directions in the**

Law of the Sea (6 vols., 1973–77). A useful general selection of the more important treaties from 1919 onwards is M. O. Hudson's International Legislation (9 vols., 1931–1950). The texts of the major recent treaties are reproduced in the bi-monthly International Legal Materials (1962–date), and some such treaties are published by HMSO as command papers. These unofficial collections sometimes omit the technical annexes to treaties, but unlike official series will include treaties before they enter into force.

8-5.   *Finding Treaty Law*

You may, for example, wish to find all the treaties on a given subject, or the treaties concluded by a certain state, or to identify the states party to a given treaty. All such questions can be answered by having recourse to an appropriate index. For many multilateral treaties the series of annual Lists of Signatures, Ratifications, Accessions, etc., for Multilateral Treaties in Respect of which the Secretary-General Performs Depository Functions, published by the United Nations, will provide the answer. This gives lists of the dates of accession or withdrawal, and the texts of reservations made, regarding all such treaties. The volume also includes the texts of declarations accepting the jurisdiction of the International Court of Justice. Treaties which are deposited with some other body, for example the Council of Europe, will be found in similar lists issued by those bodies. More comprehensive are the Indexes to the United Nations Treaty Series, which are issued from time to time and which usually cover about 50 or 100 volumes of the UNTS. These indices list action (such as accession, withdrawal or amendment) of all treaties, both bi- and multi-lateral, in the UNTS and have sections arranged chronologically, by subject, and by states party to the treaty. The LNTS has a similar set of indices. For British treaties, the Index to British Treaties (1101–1968), ed. C. Parry and C. Hopkins, (3 vols., 1970) performs the same function, again listing treaties chronologically, by subject, and by states party to it. The Index is supplemented by the Indices to the United Kingdom Treaty Series, being occasional volumes in the UKTS which are themselves frequently up-dated by supplementary lists of ratifications, etc., also published as volumes in the series. A most useful addition to treaty indices is the **World Treaty Index**, ed P. H. Rohn (5 vols., 1974), which lists treaties from the **LNTS, UNTS** and twenty-five national collections in the same three-way breakdown. Volume 1 of this series gives full details on its use. It is comprehensively cross-indexed to official treaty series, so enabling the text of the treaty to be found without difficulty. A great deal of information not readily available elsewhere is to be found in **Treaties in Force**, the annual index to United States treaties, published by the United States Department of State. Recent actions by states regarding treaties to which the United States is a party are listed in the monthly (formerly weekly) **Department of State Bulletin** and are reproduced in the bi-monthly **International Legal Materials**. Notes of such action will also be found in the **Bulletin of Legal Developments**, which deals with all major treaties, whether or not the United States is party. These sources allow up-dating of information in annual and occasional indices.

8-6.   CUSTOMARY INTERNATIONAL LAW

8-7.   *Archives*

In the absence of applicable treaty rules, the rules of customary law determine the rights and duties of States. The search for customary rules is always based on a search into the practice of States in the conduct of their international relations (para. 8-1). This practice is recorded in the various government archives, but, with the notable exception of the United States, these are often inaccessible until many years after the period to which the documents relate, to preserve official secrecy. The British archives are housed in the Public Record Office at Kew, London, and are described in a number of official guides, of which the most useful is likely to be **The Records of the Foreign Office, 1782–1939** (HMSO, 1969). Sometimes states will issue explanations of their practice, as did the United Kingdom after the *Torrey Canyon* disaster of 1967 (Cmnd. 3246, 1967). These are published as official documents, such as the series of diplomatic Blue Books, and usually in the

United Kingdom as Command Papers. Much other information will be found in Parliamentary Debates.

8-8.   *Digests*

Several states publish selections from their archives, reproducing diplomatic exchanges, opinions of governmental legal advisers, and judicial pronouncements on international law, for example. The most valuable are the United States **Digests of International Law**, beginning with that edited by J. B. Moore (8 vols., 1906) succeeded by G. H. Hackworth (8 vols., 1940–44) and finally M. M. Whiteman (15 vols., 1963–74). This series is up-dated in the new **Digest of U.S. Practice in International Law** (ed. A. Rovine) published annually since 1973, and in the "Contemporary Practice" section of the **American Journal of International Law**.

The projected **British Digest of International Law** (ed. C. Parry 1965–) is at present only partly completed, and includes only pre-1914 material. It is supplemented by the series of **Law Officers Opinions to the Foreign Office** (ed. C. Parry) covering the period to 1939, which extends the scope of **International Law Opinions** (ed. Lord McNair, 3 vols., 1956). **Opinions on Imperial Constitutional Law** (ed. D. P. O'Connell and A. Riordan, 1971) contains much valuable evidence of British views on questions of international law arising within the Empire. Several other states are producing digests, notably France (*Répertoire de la Pratique Francais*, ed. A. C. Kiss, 1962–1969) and Italy (*La Prassi Italiana Di Diritto Internazionale* (1970–date)).

8-9.   *Current Practice*

Current practice is recorded in a number of periodicals, in addition to the **American Journal of International Law**. Most comprehensive is the section entitled "Chronique des Faits" in the **Revue Générale de Droit International Public** (1894–date) although most other international law journals and particularly the various national **Yearbooks of International Law**, have sections recording recent developments in treaty law and state practice. Documents relating to major developments in state practice and selected municipal legislation are often reproduced in **International Legal Materials**. In addition, the **United Nations**

Legislative Series collects national legislation, etc., on selected topics such as nationality and the law of the sea. Some other bodies have specialised legislative series, for example, the International Labour Organisation and World Health Organisation.

Important decisions of municipal courts on any aspect of international law are reproduced in the **International Law Reports**, which carries on the series begun in 1919 under the title of the **Annual Digest of Public International Law Cases**. Sometimes cases of relevance to international lawyers are collected together by state (*e.g.* **British International Law Cases** (1963–date) and **Commonwealth International Law Cases** (1973–date), ed. Parry and Hopkins; **American International Law Cases** (1971–date), ed. F. Deak) or by subject (*e.g.* **Cases on the Law of the Sea** (1976–date), ed. K. R. Simmonds).

Great care must be taken in handling municipal laws as evidence of state practice since both statute law and common law are often applied far more restrictively than their terms suggest. For example, some provisions of the Customs Act 1876 are wide enough to apply to foreign vessels beyond the British territorial seas but no such provision has been so applied since 1850 because the British view is that such application would be contrary to international law.

State practice on a given matter will often be collected in pleadings before international tribunals, notably in the series of **Pleadings before the International Court**, as well as in periodical literature and monographs. However, it must be emphasised that the validity of the inference of rules of customary law depends upon the exhaustiveness of the survey of practice: unlike a municipal lawyer, the international lawyer can never end his search for customary law by the discovery of a binding precedent. There are cases where inadequately researched "rules" have been handed down from jurist to jurist although they had no legal basis, and cases where the practice of the European and American states (and mainly Britain and the United States), on which many writers have relied almost exclusively, diverges from that of the majority of states in the world. Comprehensive research ranging beyond the practice of the "Western" world is the only safeguard against such errors.

There are also collections of materials not selected solely on the criterion of their relevance to international law, but nevertheless often containing much material of legal interest. The **Foreign Relations of the United States** covering the period from 1861 and the **British and Foreign State Papers** covering the period from 1812, are among the continuing series of this kind, which are published by many states. Such series are often to be found in the history or politics sections of libraries. The statements of delegates to international conferences will often illustrate national views on questions of international law, as well as constituting the "travaux préparatoires" of conventions concluded by the conference which can be used to help in interpreting such conventions. These statements are usually found in the Proceedings of the conference, published by the organising body.

Finally, in addition to the sources of practice listed above, accounts of practice can be found in newspapers and other periodicals: *Le Monde* together with its supplement *Le Monde Diplomatique*, *Keesing's Contemporary Archives* and *The Times*, may be found particularly helpful.

See further, on the sources of customary law, *Ways and Means of Making the Evidence of Customary International Law More Readily Available*, (U.N. Sales No. 1949 V. 6) and, on the nature of customary law, H. W. A. Thirlway, *International Customary Law and Codification* (1972).

8-10.   GENERAL PRINCIPLES OF LAW

This source is controversial in its nature but it is generally accepted that in the absence of some precise rule which can be derived from state practice, international tribunals may determine issues by the application of general principles which are either implicit in the body of rules of customary international law (for example, the principles of the equality of states, and of good faith) or which are adopted in the legal systems of the generality of states (for example, the admissibility of circumstantial evidence). The former category represents broad principles abstracted from rules of international law, and the latter category represents broad principles widely accepted throughout the "civilised" legal systems of the world. This latter category of principles will therefore be found by searching various municipal laws: it differs from customary law in that the principles need not relate to international practice. See further on this topic B. Cheng, *General Principles of Law as applied by International Courts and Tribunals* (1953) and H. Lauterpacht, *Private Law Sources and Analogies in International Law* (1927).

8-11. JUDICIAL DECISIONS AND THE WRITINGS OF PUBLICISTS

8-12.   *Judicial Decisions*

Unlike the three previous categories, this is not a source of law in the sense that judges or publicists can create rules of law, but only evidence of the existence of rules of law. Its value therefore depends upon the accuracy with which the judges or publicists have defined the rule in question, having established its existence in one of the ways described above. Furthermore, there is no system of binding precedents in general international law, although international tribunals are naturally reluctant to depart from principles which they have laid down in earlier cases.

The most persuasive judicial decisions are, of course, those of international tribunals. The **Reports of the Permanent Court of International Justice**, and of its successor the **International Court of Justice** are pre-eminent. These two series have been rendered down into separate paragraphs, rearranged under various subject headings so as to give ready access to the jurisprudence of the Court on particular topics, in the series **The Case Law of the International Court** (ed. E. Hambro and A. W. Rovine 1952–date). Considerable weight is also attached to the awards of many international arbitral tribunals, especially where the award is made by an eminent lawyer. Some awards appear in the **International Law Reports** but the most complete collection is the series of **United Nations Reports of International Arbitral Awards**, covering the period from 1902. Earlier awards are collected in A. de Lapradelle and N. Politis, **Recueil des Arbitrages Internationaux** (3 vols., 1905–54), covering the period 1798–1875, and two collections edited by J. B. Moore, **International Adjudications** (1491–1504 and 1798–1817) (published 1929–36) and **Digest of International Arbitrations to which the United States has been a Party** (6 vols., 1898). There are also a number of volumes on arbitration before specific Commissions, for example the often-cited **Venezuelan Arbitrations of 1903** (ed. J. H. Ralston, 1904), and J. B. Scott's **Hague Court Reports** (1916, 1932). A. M. Stuyt's **Survey of International Arbitrations** 1794–1970 (1972) is a useful source of information on such arbitrations.

Opinions of municipal tribunals on questions of international law are generally given less weight, if only because such tribunals have less experience in handling international law. The major decisions are published in the **International Law Reports**, and other cases will be found in the various national reports. The **Bibliography on Foreign and Comparative Law** (1955–date) and **Guide to Foreign Legal Materials** (1959), both by C. Szladits, may be helpful. It should be noted that the role of municipal decisions here is confined to providing evidence of international law rather than as an element in state practice creating international law.

8-13.   *Publicists*

The writings of publicists are a further evidence of rules of law. Their value depends upon the esteem in which the writer is held. A list of the major treatises on the subject will be found in Vol. II of D. P. O'Connell's **International Law** (2nd ed. 1970), itself a highly regarded work. Additionally, articles in periodicals on specific topics often disclose thorough examinations of points of international law. The leading academic periodicals on international law in general are the *Recueil des Cours* (1923–date) of the Hague Academy of International Law, the *American Journal of International Law* (1907–date), the *International & Comparative Law Quarterly* (1952–date), the *Revue Générale de Droit International Public* (1894–date), and the various *Yearbooks of International Law*, such as those of Britain, Italy, Japan and the Netherlands. There are, however, valuable contributions in many other journals, and these are all indexed in the **Index to Legal Periodicals** (1908–date), the **Index to Foreign Legal Periodicals** (1960–date), and in the recent **Public International Law**, a quarterly bibliography (1975–date). The eminence of its members secures the UN International Law Commission a special place in international law and the *Yearbooks* of that body contain thorough surveys of the law on the topics under consideration for codification by the Commission. UNCITRAL plays a similar role in international trade law. The unofficial work of the Institute of International Law (1877–date) and the International Law Association (1873–date) towards codification, published in the *Reports* of those bodies, is also a valuable source of detailed discussion on specific aspects of the law.

8-14.　　　　　　　　UNILATERAL ACTS

While not mentioned as a source of law in Art. 38(1) of the Statute of the International Court of Justice, which sets out the factors the Court is directed to apply, in the 1976 *Manual of the International Court of Justice* "Unilateral acts of international law" are listed as an additional source of law to which the Court might have recourse (as it did in the *Nuclear Tests* case). The status of unilateral declarations, which appear to derive their legal force from the fact that they are intended to be acted on by other states, is unclear, but they will be found in the same materials as reproduce other examples of state practice.

18-15.　　　　　　　INTERNATIONAL ORGANISATIONS

For members of international organisations such as the United Nations or the International Labour Organisation, the rules adopted internally by the organisation, under the authority of its constitutive treaty, are a further source of obligation which may in some cases be very similar to a form of international legislation. Lawyers may wish to discover such obligations, or trace the consideration of a certain topic through the proceedings of an organisation.

The arrangement of the committees of various organisations is too complex to describe here. However, students will find the **Guide to the Use of United Nations Documents**, by B. Brimmer, L. R. Wall, W. Chamberlin and T. Hovet Jr. (1962) useful. Much valuable information for lawyers is found in the **Repertory of Practice of United Nations Organs** and its

Supplements, the **Repertoire of Practice of the Security Council** and its Supplements, the annual **United Nations Yearbook** and **United Nations Juridical Yearbook**, and the **Yearbook of the International Court of Justice.** Many other international organisations, both within and outside the United Nations "family," publish regular accounts of their work. Commonly encountered examples are the **Yearbook of the European Convention on Human Rights** and other publications of the European Commission and Court of Human Rights.

8-16. GENERAL

Finally, the important role of coursebooks may be mentioned. Several books bring together the most common cases and materials on international law. The leading books are those by D. J. Harris (*Cases and Materials on International Law*, 1979), and H. W. Briggs (*The Law of Nations*, 1952), but there are many others of this kind; those by W. W. Bishop (1971), J. O. Castel (1976), and W. E. Holder and G. A. Brennan (1972) are among the most comprehensive of such works. I. Brownlie's *Basic Documents in International Law* (1972) contains a selection of the most important treaties and United Nations Resolutions.

More detailed bibliographic information will be found in most textbooks, and for the serious student the study outlines in the *Manual of International Law* by G. Schwarzenberger and E. D. Brown (1976) are invaluable guides, arranged by subject, to the primary and secondary materials of international law. For more exhaustive bibliographies see the *Bibliography of International Law* by I. Delupis (1973), the *Cambridge International Law Catalogue*, ed. W. A. Steiner (1974) and the Harvard Law School *Catalogue of International Law and Relations* (1965–1967).

Extensive tables of abbreviations and citations of treaties, cases and statutes of many states are to be found in Vol. II of D. P. O'Connell's *International Law*, pp. 1127–1278 (1970).

Appendix I

ABBREVIATIONS OF REPORTS, SERIES AND PERIODICALS

This alphabetical list contains a selection of the more commonly used abbreviations in the United Kingdom, EEC, and the Commonwealth. It is not exhaustive and further information can be found in the I.A.L.S. *Manual of Legal Citations* Vols. I and II; *Index to Legal Periodicals*; *English and Empire Digest*, Cumulative Supplement, or the *Current Law Year Book*.

A.C. — Law Reports Appeal Cases 1891–
A.J. — Acta Juridica
A.J.I.L. — American Journal of International Law
A.L.J. — Australian Law Journal
A.L.R. — Australian Law Reports, formerly Argus Law Reports
A.L.R. — American Law Reports Annotated
A.S.C.L. — Annual Survey of Commonwealth Law
All E.R. — All England Law Reports 1936–date
All E. R. Rep. — All England Law Reports Reprint 1558–1935
Am. J. Comp. L. — American Journal of Comparative Law
Anglo-Am. L.R. — Anglo-American Law Review
Ann. Dig. — Annual Digest of Public International Law Cases (1919–49). (From 1950 this series has been published as the International Law Reports I.L.R.)
Ann. Survey Am. L. — Annual Survey of American Law
App. Cas. — Law Reports Appeal Cases 1875–1890
B.D.I.L. — British Digest of International Law
B.F.S.P. — British and Foreign State Papers
B.J.A.L. — British Journal of Administrative Law
B.J.L.S. — British Journal of Law and Society
B.L.R. — Business Law Review
B.T.R. — British Tax Review
B.Y.I.L. — British Yearbook of International Law
Business L.R. — Business Law Review
C.A.R. — Criminal Appeal Reports 1908–date
C.D.E. — Cahiers de Droit Européen

C.L.J. — Cambridge Law Journal
C.L.P. — Current Legal Problems
C.L.R. — Commonwealth Law Reports 1903–date (Australia)
C.M.L.R. — Common Market Law Reports 1962–date
C.M.L. Rev. — Common Market Law Review
C.P.D. — Law Reports Common Pleas Division 1875–1880
Calif. L. Rev. — California Law Review
Camb. L.J. — Cambridge Law Journal
Can. B.R. — Canadian Bar Review
Ch. — Law Reports Chancery Division 1891–date
Ch.D. — Law Reports Chancery Division 1875–1890
Colum. L. Rev. — Columbia Law Review
Com. Cas. — Commercial Cases 1895–1941
Conv.; Conv. (N.S.) — Conveyancer and Property Lawyer
Cox C.C. — Cox's Criminal Law Cases 1843–1941
Cr. App. R.; Cr. App. Rep. — Criminal Appeal Reports
    1908–date
Crim. L.R. — Criminal Law Review
D.L.R. — Dominion Law Reports 1912–date (Canada)
E.C.R. — European Court Reports
E.G. — Estates Gazette
E.L. Rev. — European Law Review
E.R. — English Reports 1220–1865
Eng. Rep. — English Reports 1220–1865
Eur. Comm. H.R. D.R. — European Commission of Human
    Rights Decisions and Reports
Eur. Court H.R. Series A Series B — European Court of Human
    Rights Series A & B
Ex.D. — Law Reports Exchequer Division 1875–1880
Fam. — Law Reports Family Division 1972–date
Grotius Trans. — Transactions of the Grotius Society
Harv. L. Rev. — Harvard Law Review
I.C.J. Rep. — International Court of Justice Reports
I.C.J.Y.B. — International Court of Justice Yearbook
I.C.L.Q. — International and Comparative Law Quarterly
I.C.R. — Industrial Cases Reports 1975–date
I.C.R. — Industrial Court Reports 1972–1974
I.J.; Ir. Jur. — Irish Jurist
I.L.J. — Industrial Law Journal

I.L.M. — International Legal Materials
I.L.Q. — International Law Quarterly
I.L.R. — International Law Reports
I.L.T. — Irish Law Times
I.R. — Irish Reports
Ind. C. Aw. — Industrial Court Awards 1919–date
J.B.L. — Journal of Business Law
J.C.L. — Journal of Criminal Law
J.C.M.S. — Journal of Common Market Studies
J. Legal Ed. — Journal of Legal Education
J.O. — Journal Officiel des Communautés Européennes
J.P. — Justice of the Peace Reports 1837–date
J.P.L. — Journal of Planning and Environment Law
J.R. — Juridical Review (Scotland)
J.S.P.T.L. — Journal of the Society of Public Teachers of Law
K.B. — Law Reports: King's Bench Division 1901–1952
K.I.R. — Knight's Industrial Reports 1966–date
L.A.G. Bul. — Legal Action Group Bulletin
L.G.R. — Knight's Local Government Reports 1903–
L.J. — Law Journal 1866–1965 (newspaper)
L.J. Adm. — Law Journal Admiralty N.S. 1865–1875
L.J. Bcy. — Law Journal Bankruptcy N.S. 1832–1880
L.J.C.C.R. — Law Journal County Courts Reporter 1912–1947
L.J.C.P. — Law Journal Common Pleas N.S. 1831–1875
L.J. Ch. — Law Journal Chancery N.S. 1831–1946
L.J. Eccl. — Law Journal Ecclesiastical Cases N.S. 1866–1875
L.J. Eq. — Law Journal, Chancery, N.S. 1831–1946
L.J. Ex. — Law Journal Exchequer N.S. 1831–1875
L.J. Ex. Eq. — Law Journal Exchequer in Equity 1835–1841
L.J.K.B. (or Q.B.) — Law Journal King's (or Queen's) Bench N.S. 1831–1946
L.J.M.C. — Law Journal Magistrates' Cases N.S. 1831–1896
L.J.N.C. — Law Journal Notes of Cases 1866–1892
L.J.N.C.C.R. — Law Journal Newspaper, County Court Reports 1934–1947
L.J.O.S. — Law Journal, Old Series 1822–1831
L.J.P. — Law Journal Probate Divorce and Admiralty N.S. 1875–1946

L.J.P.D. & A. — Law Journal Probate Divorce and Admiralty N.S. 1875–1946

L.J.P. & M. — Law Journal Probate and Matrimonial Cases N.S. 1858–1859, 1866–1875

L.J.P.C. — Law Journal Privy Council N.S. 1865–1946

L.J.P. M. & A. — Law Journal Probate, Matrimonial and Admiralty N.S. 1860–1865

L.J.R. — Law Journal Reports 1947–1949

L. Lib.J. — Law Library Journal

L.M.C.L.Q. — Lloyd's Maritime and Commercial Law Quarterly 1974–date

L.N.T.S. — League of Nations Treaty Series

L.Q.R. — Law Quarterly Review

L.R. — Law Reports 1865–date

L.R.A. & E. — Law Reports: Admiralty and Ecclesiastical Cases 1865–1875

L.R.C.C.R. — Law Reports: Crown Cases Reserved 1865–1875

L.R. C.P. — Law Reports: Common Pleas Cases 1865–1875

L.R. Ch. App. — Law Reports: Chancery Appeal Cases 1865–1875

L.R. Eq. — Law Reports: Equity Cases 1866–1875

L.R. Ex. — Law Reports: Exchequer Cases 1865–1875

L.R.H.L. — Law Reports: English and Irish Appeals 1866–1875

L.R. P. & D. — Law Reports: Probate and Divorce Cases 1865–1875

L.R.P.C. — Law Reports: Privy Council Appeals 1865–1875

L.R.Q.B. — Law Reports: Queen's Bench 1865–1875

L.R.R.P.; L.R. R.P.C. — Restrictive Practices Cases 1957–1973

L.S. Gaz. — Law Society Gazette

L.T.R.; L.T. Rep. — Law Times Reports (New Series) 1859–1947

L.T.Jo. — Law Times (newspaper) 1843–1965

L.T.O.S. — Law Times Reports, Old Series 1843–1860

L. Teach. — Law Teacher

Law & Contemp. Prob. — Law and Contemporary Problems

Ll. L.L.R.; Ll.L.R.; Ll.L. Rep. — Lloyd's List Law Reports 1919–date

Lloyd L.R.; Lloyd's Rep. — Lloyd's List Law Reports 1919–date

M.L.R. — Modern Law Review

Man. Law — Managerial Law
Mich. L. Rev. — Michigan Law Review
N.I. — Northern Ireland Law Reports
N.I.L.Q. — Northern Ireland Legal Quarterly
N.L.J. — New Law Journal
N.Y.U.L. Rev. — New York University Law Review
N.Z.L.R. — New Zealand Law Reports 1883–date
New L.J.; N.L. Jo. — New Law Journal
O.J.C. — Official Journal of the European Communities: Information and Notices
O.J.L. — Official Journal of the European Communities: Legislation: *e.g.* 1972, L 139/28
P. — Law Reports Probate, Divorce and Admiralty 1891–1971
P. & C.R. — Planning (Property from 1968) and Compensation Reports 1949–date
P.C.I.J. — Permanent Court of International Justice Reports of Judgments
P.D. — Law Reports Probate Division 1875–1890
P.L. — Public Law
Q.B. — Law Reports: Queen's Bench Division 1891–1901, 1952–date
Q.B.D. — Law Reports Queen's Bench Division 1875–1890
R.D.E. — Rivista di Dirritio Europeo
R.G.D.I.P. — Revue Générale de Droit Internationale Public
R.M.C. — Revue du Marché Commun
R.P.C. — Reports of Patent, Design & Trade Mark Cases 1884–date
R.R. — Revised Reports
R.T.R. — Road Traffic Reports 1970–date
Rec. — Recueil des Cours
Rec. — Recueil de la Jurisprudence de la Cour (Court of Justice of the European Communities)
S.A. — South African Law Reports
S.C. — Session Cases (Scotland)
S.C. (H.L.) — Session Cases (Scotland) House of Lords 1906–date
S.C.(J.) — Session Cases Justiciary Cases (Scotland) 1906–1916
S.I. — Statutory Instruments
S.I. Rev. — Statutory Rules and Orders and Statutory Instruments Revised

S.J. — Solicitors' Journal
S.L.T. — Scots Law Times 1893–date
S.T.C. — Simon's Tax Cases
Sol. Jo. — Solicitors' Journal
St. Tr.; State Tr. — State Trials 1163–1820
State Tr. N.S. — State Trials, New Series 1820–1858
T.C. — Reports of Tax Cases 1875–date
T.L.R. — Times Law Reports 1884–1952
Tax Cas. — Reports of Tax Cases 1875–date
Tul. L. Rev. — Tulane Law Review
U. Chi. L. Rev. — University of Chicago Law Review
U.K.T.S. — United Kingdom Treaty Series
U.N.T.S. — United Nations Treaty Series
U.N.J.Y. — United Nations Juridical Yearbook
U.N.Y.B.; Y.U.N. — Yearbook of the United Nations
U. Pa. L. Rev. — University of Pennsylvania Law Review
U.S. — United States Supreme Court Reports
U.S.T.S. — United States Treaty Series
W.L.R. — Weekly Law Reports 1953–date
W.N. — Weekly Notes
Y.B. — Yearbook (old law report) *e.g.* (1466) Y.B. Mich. (the term) 6 Edw. 4, pl. 18, fol.7. (plea, folio)
Y.B.W.A. — Yearbook of World Affairs
Yale L.J. — Yale Law Journal
Yearbook E.C.H.R. — Yearbook of the European Convention on Human Rights

Appendix II

WORDS AND ABBREVIATIONS IN
ENGLISH AND LATIN

This alphabetical list contains a selection of the more commonly
used legal words and abbreviations in English and Latin.

A.G. or Att. Gen. — Attorney-General
A.G. — German incorporated company
Ab Initio — from the beginning
Abstracts — summary of periodical articles, books, etc. Usually
   arranged in subject order
Ad Valorem — according to the duty. A duty levied
Aliter — otherwise
Amicus Curiae — a friend of the court (a bystander who informs the
   judge on points of law or fact)
Annotations — notes
Anon. — anonymous
Applied (apld.) — the principle in a previous case has been applied
   to a new set of facts in another case
Approved — the case has been considered good law
Article — an essay published in a journal
Autrefois acquit — previously acquitted
Autrefois attaint — previously attainted
Autrefois convict — previously convicted
B. — Baron (Exchequer)
B.C. — Borough Council
Bibliography — a list of books
Bills — draft versions of proposed legislation, laid before
   Parliament for its approval
Bl. Comm. — Blackstone, *Commentaries on the Laws of England*
Blue book — a government publication, issued with blue covers to
   protect it because of its length
c. — chapter (Act)
C. — Command Paper 1836–1899
C.A. — Court of Appeal

C.B. — Chief Baron

C.A.V. — curia advisari vult; the court deliberated before pronouncing judgment

C.C. — County Council

C.C.A. — Court of Criminal Appeal

C.C.R. — County Court Rules

c.i.f. — (Cost, insurance, freight) a contract for the sale of goods in which the price quoted includes everything up to delivery

C.J. — Chief Justice

cap. — chapter (Act)

Cd. — Command Papers 1900–1918

cf. — (confer) to compare or refer to

Chronological — arranged in order of date

Cie. — French abbreviation for company

Citation — (1) a reference to where a case or statute is to be found (2) the quotation of decided cases in legal arguments

Citator — a volume containing a list of cases or statutes with sufficient details to enable them to be traced in the volumes of law reports or statutes

Cl. — clause (in Bills)

Classification number — a system of numbers, or letters and numbers, used to indicate the subject matter of the book. In many libraries the books are arranged on the shelves in the order indicated by this number

Command Paper — a form of Parliamentary paper, issued "by Command of Her Majesty." Every Command Paper has its own individual number

Comrs. — Commissioners

Cmd. — Command Papers 1919–1956

Cmnd. — Command Papers 1956–

Co. Litt. — Coke on Littleton

Considered — the case was considered but no comment was made

Cumulative; Cumulation — combining the information in a number of previous publications into one sequence

Cur. adv. vult. — Court deliberated before pronouncing judgment

D.P.P. — Director of Public Prosecutions (whose name appears in criminal appeals to the House of Lords, and certain other circumstances)

Deb. — Debates (*i.e.* Parliamentary debates)

De facto — in fact

De jure — by right

De novo — anew

Dec. — decision (Common Market) *e.g.* Dec. 72/112/EEC

Decd. — deceased

Delegated legislation — rules created by subordinate bodies under specific powers delegated by Parliament

Digest — a summary

Digested — summarised

Dir. — Directive (Common Market) *e.g.* Dir. 72/262/EEC

Distinguished — some essential difference between past cases and the present case has been pointed out

Doe d. — (Doe on the demise of)

Doubted — court's remarks tend to show case was inaccurate

Et seq. — (et sequentes) — and those following

Ex cathedra (from the chair) — with official authority

Ex officio — by virtue of an office

Ex.p. — *ex parte* the person on whose application the case is heard

Ex post facto — by a subsequent act — retrospectively

Ex rel. — ex relatione — report not at first hand

Explained — previous decision is not doubted, but the present decision is justified by calling attention to some fact not clear in the report

f.o.b. — free on board — cost of shipping to be paid by vendor

Folio — technically this refers to the way in which a book is made up; usually used to denote a large book, often shelved in a separate sequence

Followed — same principle of law applied

GmbH. — German incorporated private company

Green Paper — a government publication setting out government proposals, so that public discussion may follow before a definite policy is formulated

H.C. Deb. — House of Commons Debate

H.L. — House of Lords

H.M.S.O. — Her Majesty's Stationery Office

Hale P.C. — Hale, *Historia Placitorum Coronae* (Pleas of the Crown)

Hansard — Parliamentary Debates

Headnote — a brief summary of a case found at the beginning of the law report

I.C.J. — International Court of Justice
I.R.C. — Inland Revenue Commissioners
Ibid. — *ibidem* — in the same place
Id. — *idem* — the same
In b. — *in bonis* — in the goods of
In camera — hearing in private
In curia — in open court
In re — in the matter of
Infra — below
Inter alia — amongst other things
Inter vivos — during life: between living persons
Ipso facto — by the mere fact
J. (plural JJ.) — judge
K.C. — King's Counsel
L.B.C. — London Borough Council
L.C. — Lord Chancellor
L.C.B. — Lord Chief Baron
L.C.J. — Lord Chief Justice
L.J. — Lord Justice (plural L. JJ.)
Legislation — the making of law: any set of statutes
Loc.cit. — *loco citato* — at the passage quoted
M.R. — Master of the Rolls
M.V. — motor vessel
Microfiche; Microfilm — a photographic reduction of an original
    onto a sheet of film (microfiche) or a reel of film (microfilm). A
    reading machine (which enlarges the image) is needed to consult
    microfilm or fiche
N.S. — new series
N.V. — Dutch incorporated company
Nisi prius — unless before
Nolle prosequi — unwilling to prosecute
Non-Parliamentary papers — Government publications which are
    not required to be laid before Parliament for their approval.
    They are usually entered in the library catalogue under the name
    of the government department which publishes them
O.S. — old series
Obiter dictum — a judicial observation on a point not directly
    relevant to the case (not binding as precedent)
Op.cit. — the book previously cited

Orse — otherwise

Overruled — a higher court holds the decision to be wrong

P.C. — Privy Council

P.C.I.J. — Permanent Court of International Justice

Pace — by permission of

Pamphlet — a small booklet usually less than 50 pages in length. It may be shelved in a separate sequence

Parl. Deb. — Parliamentary Debates

Pari Passu — on an equal footing, or proportionately

Parliamentary Papers — papers required by Parliament in the course of their work. These include: House of Lords and House of Commons Papers and Bills, Debates, Command Papers and Acts

Per — as stated by

Per curiam — a decision arrived at by the court

Per incuriam — through want of care (a mistaken court decision)

Periodical — a publication with a distinctive title which appears regularly

Periodicals index — (1) an index to the contents of a particular journal (2) a subject index to articles in a number of journals

Per pro — per procurationem — as an agent — on behalf of another

Per se — by itself — taken alone

Post — after (a later line or page)

Q.C. — Queen's Counsel

q.v. — *quod vide* — which see

Quantum meruit — as much as he had earned/deserved

r. — rule

R.( ) — Decision of administrative tribunal — letter in brackets indicates the appropriate tribunal

R v. — Rex, Regina (the King, Queen) against

R.S.C. Ord. — Rules of the Supreme Court, Order

Ratio decidendi — the ground of a decision

Re — in the matter of

Rec. — Recueil

Reg. — Regina (the Queen)

Reg. — Regulations (Common Market) *e.g.* Reg. 467/72/EEC

Regnal year — the year of the monarch's reign

s. — section (plural ss.)

S.A. — French company

S.C. — same case
S.G. — Solicitor-General
S.I. — Statutory Instrument
S.R. & O. — Statutory Rules and Orders
SS. — steamship
Sched. — schedule (Act)
Scienter — knowingly
Semble — it appears
Sessional Papers — a collection of all Parliamentary Papers published during a particular session of Parliament
Sessional set — a collection of all Parliamentary papers issued during a particular session of Parliament, bound up into volumes
Statutes — Acts of Parliament
Sub judice — in course of trial
Sub nom. — *sub nomine* — under the name
Sub voce. — under the title
Supra — above
T.S. — Treaty series
Table of cases/statutes — a list of cases or statutes in alphabetical order
Treaty — (1) negotiations prior to an agreement (2) an agreement between nations
U.D.C. — Urban District Council
Ultra vires — beyond the power
Union catalogue/union list — a catalogue of the contents of a number of libraries (*e.g.* all the libraries in a university)
v. — versus
V.C. — Vice-Chancellor
Venire de novo — motion for a new trial
Viz. — *videlicet* — namely: that is to say
White Book — a term sometimes used to refer to the Supreme Court Practice
White Paper — a Parliamentary paper, usually containing a statement of government policy

Appendix III

HOW DO I FIND? A SUMMARY OF SOURCES

ABBREVIATIONS (1–8; 2–12)

Where to Look for Your Law.

Sweet & Maxwell's Guide to Law Reports and Statutes.

University of London Institute of Advanced Legal Studies — *Manual of Legal Citations.*

The front pages of: *Current Law Case Citator; Current Law Citator; English and Empire Digest,* Vol. 1, and the Cumulative Supplement; *Index to Legal Periodicals; Halsbury's Laws of England,* Vol. 1.

Osborn's Concise Law Dictionary, (6th ed., 1976) pp. 353 *et seq.*

Price and Bitner, *Effective Legal Research* (for American abbreviations).

List in Appendix I.

BOOKS

TRACING BOOKS ON A SUBJECT

Consult the **Subject Index** to the library catalogue, then look in the **Subject (or Classified) Catalogue** under the numbers, or letters and numbers, given in the Subject Index. (6–32)

Consult BIBLIOGRAPHIES (see below).

TRACING BOOKS BY AN AUTHOR

Consult the library's **Author (or Name) Catalogue** (1–4)

Consult BIBLIOGRAPHIES (see below).

TRACING BOOKS IF YOU KNOW THE TITLE

If your library's catalogue does not contain entries under titles, consult BIBLIOGRAPHIES (see below) to find the author's name, then consult the Author Catalogue.

Appendix III

BIBLIOGRAPHIES

Raistrick and Rees, *Lawyers' Law Books* (entries under subjects). (6–38)

Law Books in Print (entries under authors, titles and subjects). (6–35)

Law Books Published (entries under authors, titles, subjects). (6–34)

Current Publications in Legal and Related Fields (authors, titles, subjects). (6–37)

Current Law and *Current Law Year Books* (entries under subjects). (6–9, 6–10, 6–36)

Chloros, *Bibliographical Guide to the Law of the United Kingdom* (guide to the main textbooks in each subject). (6–38)

Legal Bibliography of the British Commonwealth (useful for older books). (6–38)

Bibliography on Foreign and Comparative Law. (6–38)

British National Bibliography (British books, on all subjects, published since 1950. Entries under authors, titles, subjects). (6–40)

British Books in Print (entries under authors, titles). (6–40)

Books in Print (American books in print — authors, titles, and separate *Subject Guide to Books in Print*). (6–40)

Cumulative Book Index (Books in English published throughout the world — entries under authors, titles, subjects). (6–40)

Specialist legal bibliographies (6–38) — Ask the library staff for advice.

The Catalogues of large specialist and national libraries *e.g. British Museum General Catalogue of Printed Books; Library of Congress Catalog,* etc. (6–40)

CASES

IF YOU KNOW THE NAME OF THE CASE (summary pp. 40-41)

Current Law Case Citator and *Current Law Citator,* (2–14)

English and Empire Digest (for English, Scottish, Irish and Commonwealth cases of any date). Consult Volumes 52 to 54 and the Cumulative Supplement (for cases after 1966). (2–15)

Law Reports: Consolidated Indexes. (2–16)

163

English Reports, Vols. 177–178 (for English cases *before 1865*). (2–10)
All England Law Reports Consolidated Tables and Index 1936–date, and *All English Law Reports Reprint Index,* 1558–1935. (2–16, 2–11)

FOR VERY RECENT CASES

Latest month's issue of *Current Law* — the cumulative table of cases. (2–17, 6–9)
Latest "pink" index to The Law Reports *and* the latest issue of the *Weekly Law Reports* (index of cases reported). (2–17)
Current Cumulative Tables and Index to the All England Law Reports. (2–17)
Cases in recent copies of *The Times.*
Summaries of cases in weekly journals, *e.g. Solicitors Journal; New Law Journal; Law Society Gazette.* (2–17)

SCOTTISH CASES

Scottish Current Law Citators. (2–14)
English and Empire Digest. (2–15)

IRISH CASES

Irish Digests.
Index to Northern Ireland Cases.
English and Empire Digest. (2–15)

COMMONWEALTH CASES

English and Empire Digest. (2–15)

TRACING CASES ON A SUBJECT (6–8)

English and Empire Digest. (6–12)
Current Law Year Book 1976, latest *Current Law Year Book,* and latest monthly issue of *Current Law.* (6–9, 6–10)
Halsbury's Laws of England. (6–3)
Law Reports: Consolidated Indexes. (6–13)

Appendix III

TRACING THE SUBSEQUENT JUDICIAL HISTORY OF A CASE (6–14)

Current Law Citator, Current Law Case Citator and latest monthly issue of *Current Law* (for cases judicially considered after 1947). (6–14)

English and Empire Digest. (6–11)

Law Reports: Consolidated Indexes (table of cases judicially considered). (6–13)

All England Law Reports: Consolidated Tables and Index (cases reported and considered). (6–13)

ARE THERE ANY PERIODICAL ARTICLES ON THIS CASE?

Current Law Citator and *Current Law Case Citator* (entries enclosed in square brackets are periodical articles). (2–14, 2–18)

Latest issue of *Current Law* (entries in italics in the cumulative table of cases indicate cases judicially considered or periodical articles on that case). (2–18)

Index to Legal Periodicals (table of cases commented upon, at the back of the volume). (2–18)

Indexes to individual periodicals, *e.g. Modern Law Review; Law Quarterly Review.*

CITATIONS

Government publications. (5–5, 5–8, 5–10, 5–11)

Law reports in general. (2–4)

The Law Reports. (2–8)

Statutes. (3–3, 3–22)

Statutory Instruments. (3–26)

DIRECTORIES

Law List 1976. (1–12)

Bar List of the United Kingdom. (1–12)

Solicitors Diary and Directory. (1–12)

GENERAL STATEMENTS OF THE LAW

Textbooks. Consult the library catalogues and Bibliographies (see entry under BOOKS) to trace relevant publications.

Halsbury's Laws of England. (6–3)
Specialised legal encyclopedias. (6–6)

GOVERNMENT PUBLICATIONS

TRACING PUBLICATIONS ON A SUBJECT (5–22, 6–41)

Consult the subject index to the library's government publications collection, if one exists.
Consult monthly, annual and five-yearly catalogues of *Government Publications.* (5–14)
Sectional Lists of Government Publications. (5–22)
Breviates of Parliamentary papers (for older publications). (5–25)
Irish Universities Press reprints of nineteenth century government publications (each volume, or set of volumes, deals with one subject). (5–25)
Current Law and *Current Law Year Books.* (6–9, 6–10)
Lawyers' Law Books includes the main government reports on each subject. (6–38)

INDEXES TO GOVERNMENT PUBLICATIONS

Daily List of Government Publications. (5–14)
Government Publications (monthly, annual and five-yearly). (5–14)
General Index . . . 1900–1949. (5–14)

IF YOU KNOW THE NAME OF THE CHAIRMAN OF A REPORT

Richard, *British Government Publications; an Index to Chairmen and Authors, 1900–1940.* (5–20)
Morgan, *British Government Publications; an index to Chairmen and Authors, 1941–1966.* (5–20)
Index to Chairmen of Committees (published quarterly by HMSO). (5–20)
Monthly, annual and five-yearly indexes to *Government Publications.* (5–14)

LAW COMMISSION REPORTS AND WORKING PAPERS

The Law Commission's annual reports (issued as House of Commons Papers) include a complete list of all the Law

Commission reports and working papers, showing whether the recommendations of each report have been implemented. (5–24)

Daily List, and the monthly and annual catalogues of *Government Publications* include new Law Commission reports as they are published. (5–14)

PERIODICAL ARTICLES

ARTICLES ON A SUBJECT

Index to Legal Periodicals. (4–4)

Index to Foreign Legal Periodicals. (4–5)

Current Law (under appropriate subject heading) (6–9) and *Current Law Year Books* (at the back of the volumes). (4–3, 6–10)

Annual Abridgment to Halsbury's Laws of England (under appropriate subject heading) and the *Monthly Reviews* (in the looseleaf Service Volume). (4–6, 6–5)

Index to Periodical Articles Relating to Law. (4–8)

British Humanities Index. (4–9)

Other non-legal periodical indexes. (4–10 *et seq,*)

ARTICLES ON A CASE

Current Law Citator and *Current Law Case Citator* (entries enclosed in square brackets are periodical articles). (2–14, 2–18)

Latest monthly issue of *Current Law* (entries in italics in the cumulative table of cases). (2–18)

Index to Legal Periodicals (table of cases commented upon). (2–18)

For recent cases, look through the editorial comments in weekly journals, *e.g. Solicitors Journal, New Law Journal, Justice of the Peace,* and specialist periodicals, *e.g. Criminal Law Review.*

ARTICLES ON AN ACT

Current Law Statute Citator 1947—1971 and the statute citator in the latest *Current Law Citator.* (6–25)

Indexes to periodicals (under the appropriate subject heading).

TRACING PERIODICALS

Consult the library's **Periodicals Catalogue,** if there is one. (1–9)

If the periodical is not available in your library, consult the *Union*

List of Legal Periodicals (4–18) to find out where a copy is available.

Union lists of the periodicals available in your own area or region may be available – ask the library staff for advice.

STATUTES

COLLECTIONS OF THE STATUTES

Older Statutes

Statutes of the Realm. (3–17)

Statutes at Large (various editions). (3–18)

Firth and Rait, *Acts and Ordinances of the Interregnum.* (3–19)

Statutes Revised (statutes in force in 1948). (3–20)

Modern Statutes

Public General Acts and Measures. (3–7)

Law Reports: Statutes. (3–10)

Current Law Statutes Annotated. (3–12)

Statutes in Force. (6–17)

Butterworth's Annotated Legislation Service. (3–13)

Halsbury's Statutes. (3–14, 6–19)

Collections of Acts by subject

Statutes in Force. (6–17)

Halsbury's Statutes. (6–19)

Annotated editions of the Statutes

Current Law Statutes. (3–12)

Butterworth's Annotated Legislation Service. (3–13)

Halsbury's Statutes. (3–14, 6–19)

Statutes in Force

Statutes in Force. (6–17)

Index to the Statutes. (6–18)

Statutes Revised (statutes in force in 1948). (3–20)

Halsbury's Statutes. (3–14, 6–19, 6–23)

Chronological Table of the Statutes. (6–24)

Current Law Statute Citator and *Current Law Citator.* (6–25)

TRACING STATUTES ON A SUBJECT

Statutes in Force. (6–17)

Halsbury's Statutes. (6–19)

Appendix III

Index to Statutes. (6–18)
Halsbury's Laws. (6–9)
Current Law and *Current Law Year Books.* (6–9, 6–10)

INDEXES TO THE STATUTES

Chronological Table of the Statutes (shows whether Acts of any date are still in force). (6–24)
Index to the Statutes (alphabetically arranged by subject, and lists all the Acts dealing with that subject). (6–18)
Halsbury's Statutes (alphabetically arranged by subject. Consult Index to Volumes 1–45 and the Cumulative Supplement to check if an Act is still in force). (6–23)
Public General Acts: Tables and Index (annual — brings the information in the *Chronological Table of Statutes* up to date). (6–24)

LOCAL AND PERSONAL ACTS – INDEXES

Index to Local and Personal Acts 1801–1947. (3–23)
Supplementary Index to the Local and Personal Acts 1948–1966. (3–23)
Local and Personal Acts; Tables and Index (annually). (3–23)

IS THIS ACT STILL IN FORCE? HAS IT BEEN AMENDED?

Chronological Table of the Statutes (indicates if an Act of any date is in force). (6–24)
Public General Acts: Tables and Index (annually — brings the information in the Chronological Table up to date — see the table "Effects of Legislation"). (6–24)
Halsbury's Statutes (consult the Index to Volumes 1–45, the Cumulative Supplement *and* the looseleaf Service under the heading "Statutory Instrument Appointing Days"). (6–23)
Current Law Statute Citator and *Current Law Citator.* (6–25)

WHAT CASES HAVE THERE BEEN ON THE INTERPRETATION OF THIS ACT?

Current Law Statute Citator and *Current Law Citator.* (6–25)
Halsbury's Statutes. (6–19)

WHAT STATUTORY INSTRUMENTS HAVE BEEN MADE UNDER THIS ACT?
Current Law Statute Citator and *Current Law Citator*. (6–25)
Index to Government Orders. (6–28)
Halsbury's Statutes. (6–19)

HAVE ANY PERIODICAL ARTICLES BEEN WRITTEN ABOUT THIS ACT?
Current Law Statute Citator and *Current Law Citator*. (6–25)
Indexes to periodical articles (see PERIODICAL ARTICLES, above) under appropriate subject heading.

HAS THIS ACT BEEN BROUGHT INTO FORCE BY A STATUTORY INSTRUMENT?

Halsbury's Statutes (Current Statutes Service). (6–23)
Current Law Statute Citator, Current Law Citator and Current Law. (6–25)

STATUTORY INSTRUMENTS

COLLECTIONS OF STATUTORY INSTRUMENTS

Statutory Rules and Orders and Statutory Instruments Revised (all statutory instruments in force in 1948). (3–27)
Statutory Instruments (annual volumes — subject index in last volume of each year). (3–27)
Halsbury's Statutory Instruments (selective — arranged by subject). (6–27)

IS THIS STATUTORY INSTRUMENT IN FORCE? HAS IT BEEN AMENDED?

Statutory Rules and Orders and Statutory Instruments Revised (a collection of statutory instruments in force in 1948, arranged by subject). (3–27)
Table of Government Orders (indicates for every statutory instrument whether it is still in force). (6–31)
Halsbury's Statutory Instruments. (6–27)
List of Statutory Instruments (monthly and annually). (3–27)

Appendix III

WHAT STATUTORY INSTRUMENTS HAVE BEEN MADE UNDER THIS
ACT? (6–30)

Current Law Statute Citator and *Current Law Citator.* (6–25)
Index to Government Orders. (6–28)
Halsbury's Statutes. (6–19)

HAS THIS ACT BEEN BROUGHT INTO FORCE BY A STATUTORY
INSTRUMENT?

Halsbury's Statutes (Current Statutes Service). (6–23)
Current Law Statute Citator, Current Law Citator and Current Law.
(6–25)

INDEXES TO STATUTORY INSTRUMENTS

Table of Government Orders (chronological, showing whether each
Instrument is still in force). (6–31)
Index to Government Orders (arranged by subject). (6–28)
Halsbury's Statutory Instruments (by subject). (6–27)
Lists of Statutory Instruments (monthly and annually — entries by
subject, and under the numbers of the Instruments). (6–29)
Daily List of Government Publications (includes all new Instruments
as they are published). (6–29)

WORDS AND PHRASES

For the meaning of words and phrases use legal **Dictionaries**.
(1–12)
For Latin phrases use legal dictionaries and Broom's *Legal Maxims.*
(1–12)

JUDICIAL AND STATUTORY DEFINITIONS OF WORDS AND PHRASES

Words and Phrases Legally Defined. (6–15)
Stroud's Judicial Dictionary. (6–15)
The entry "words and phrases" in: *Law Reports; Consolidated Indexes;
Current Law and Current Law Year Books;* the Indexes to the *All
England Law Reports; Halsbury's Laws* (3rd ed.), General Index;
English and Empire Digest, Consolidated Index.

Appendix IV

ANSWERS TO PROBLEMS

29   (a) [1929] 712
        [1558 –1774] 497
        Ultzen v. *Nicols* [1891– 4] 1202

      (b) *R.* v. *Porter*
        Scott v. *Inland Revenue Commissioners*
        Langley v. *Fisher*

33   (1884) 26 Ch. D. 66
        The Times, May 12, 1953
        (1967) 111 S.J. 122; 117 New L.J. 74

38   (1825) 5 Russ. 13, n; 38 E.R. 932
        (1849) 13 Q.B. 840; 13 L.T.O.S. 527; 116 E.R. 1484
        [1975] 2 All E.R. 282; [1975] 1 W.L.R. 1587; 119
        Sol. Jo. 760

43   25 *Modern Law Review* 1; 77 *Law Quarterly Review* 175,
        179; 105 *Solicitors Journal* 69; 34 *Australian Law
        Journal* 317; [1961] *Journal of Business Law* 252; 111
        Law Journal 609, 624; 95 *Irish Law Times* 213, 219,
        225; 78 *South African Law Journal* 293; 4 *Sydney Law
        Review* 99; [1963] *Osgoode Hall Law Journal* 416

49   (a) Community Land Act
      (b) 1971 c. 78
      (c) Solicitors Act 1957
      (d) 12 & 13 Geo. 6, c. 68
        12, 13 & 14 Geo. 6
      (e) 1936
        1937
        The volume contains the statutes passed in the
        Parliamentary Session which ran from November
        1936 to October 1937: See explanation at para. 3-3.

56   (a) Grants by Local Authorities Order 1977
      (b) Extradition (Protection of Aircraft) (Amendment) Order
        S.I. 1976/770
      (c) An explanation of the meaning of the instrument
        No

61   (a) O.P. Wylie
       (b) Criminal L.R. 200

63   (a) (i) Physicians and Surgeons
           (ii) Natural Resources
       (b) "Law-creative role of appellate courts in developing
           countries: an emphasis on East Africa" (1975) 24
           International and Comparative Law Quarterly 205–54
       (c) O. Lang

63   (a) United Kingdom
           United States
           Sweden
       (b) Review of Ghana Law

64   M.D.J. Groom

65   "Poverty and the Law — the Limitations of Australian
       Legal Aid"

80   (a) Two
       (b) Mr Deakins
       (c) [891] 1604–5
           Mr Freud
           The age of the child

83   (a) Report on the Work of the Prison Department 1974
       (b) [155]
           House of Commons Bill
           Session 1974–75
       (c) Contempt of Court
       (d) Cmnd. 5794
       (e) Law Com. No. 60, Cmnd. 5709
       (f) Congenital Disabilities (Civil Liability) Act 1976
       (g) Home Office

92   (a) Vol. 36, third edition
       (b) pp. 51–52; para. 72
       (c) [1972] 2 All E.R. 1192

None at present
(d) "The Legal Status of Articled Clerks" D. Rose, 120 Sol.Jo. 671
(e) 4th ed.
    Vol. XI, para. 1243
(f) No.
    Endangered Species (Import and Export) Act 1976
(g) Vol. 12, Deeds
(h) Maximum fine increased to £500 by Criminal Law Act 1977, s. 31, Sched. 6

99   (a) *Baker* v. *Jones*; *Martell* v. *Consett Iron Co.*; *Clyne* v. *Bar Association of New South Wales*; *William Hill (Park Lane)* v. *Sunday Pictorial Newspapers*; *Hill* v. *Archbold*
      (b) *R.* v. *Semini* [1949] 1 K.B. 405
      (c) Hijacking Act 1971; Extradition (Hijacking) Order 1971; Extradition (Hijacking) (Amendment) Order 1975

106   (a) Vol. 19
          Vol. 35
      (b) Vol. 43, page 97, 831–1151

110   Succession, 5
      Property, England and Wales, 1

113   (a) Rabies Act 1974
      (b) Yes, S.I. 1977 No. 361
      (c) Criminal Law Act

118   Subsection (1) is amended by the Adoption Act 1976 s. 73(2), Sched. 3 para 19, as from a day to be appointed.

119   No. Repealed by the Trustee Investments Act 1961, c. 62, s. 16(2), Sched. 5

121   (a) 1973 c. 55
      (b) *R.* v. *Feely, Edwards* v. *Ddin, R.* v. *McHugh, Pilgram* v. *Rice-Smith*

122 (a) Air Navigation (Restriction of Flying) (Atomic Energy Establishments) Regulations 1976/1986
(b) Aldermaston, Calder /Windscale, Capenhurst, Chapel-cross, Coulport, Dounreay, Harwell, Springfields, Winfrith
(c) Oil Cake Welfare Order 1929; Beer Regulations 1952

123 (a) 1967/292
(b) Agriculture (Miscellaneous Provisions) Act 1954 (c. 39), s.10

127 (a) Constitutional and administrative law
(b) Hill, Larry B.; *Model Ombudsman: Institutionalising New Zealand's Democratic Experiment*

128 Item 2807 — Simon, Frances H. *Field Wing Bail Hostel; the first nine months*

128 (b) Bunyan, T. *The History and Practice of Political Police in Britain*
Hedley, P. & Aynsley, C. *The "D" Notice Affair*
Prime Minister: *The "D" Notice System* (Cmnd. 3312)
Privy Council: *Report of the Committee of Privy Councillors appointed to Inquire into "D" Notice Matters* (Cmnd. 3309)

131 (a) 347.42016
(b) Harrison, Brian Fraser, and Chislett, Albert John
(c) Shaw & Sons
£2.00
(d) Stein, Peter
Edinburgh University Press
(e) "No fault on the roads"
Kohl, Marvin, *The Morality of Killing: Sanctity of Life, abortion and euthanasia*. London: Owen, 1974

137 (a) Council Regulation EEC No. 2595/77
(b) Reg. 1408/71 J.O. 1971, L 149/2 and Reg. 574/72 J.O. 1972, L 74/1

138   (a) Case 2/74 *Reyners* v. *Belgium*
       (b) Rec. 1965, 89; [1962] E.C.R. 45; [1962] C.M.L.R. 1

139   (a) H. H. Maas
       (b) A. C. Page

Index

Index

Index

Index

(index)

Scottish Current Law. See Current Law.
Social Sciences Index, 4–10
Sociological Abstracts, 4–15
Solicitors' Diary and Directory, the, 1–11
Solicitor's Journal, the, 2–3
Specialised encyclopedias, 6–6
Standing committee debates, official reports of, 5–7
Statutes at Large, 3–18
Statutes in Force, 6–17
Statutes of the Realm, 3–17
Statutes Revised, the, 3–20
Statutory Instruments, 3–24 *et seq.*
  list of, 3–27
Statutory Instruments Revised, 3–27
Statutory Rules and Orders, 3–27
Stroud's Judicial Dictionary, 6–15
Students' Law Reporter, the, 2–18
Subordinate legislation. See Delegated legislation.
Supreme Court Practice, the, 6–7
Sweet & Maxwell's Guide to the Law Reports and Statutes, 1–8

Textbooks, reserve or short-term loan, 1–3
The Times, European Law Reports, 7–4
  Index to, 4–16
  recent reports in, 2–5
Treaties in Force, 8–5

Union List of Legal Periodicals, 4–18
United Nations Treaty Series, 8–3
United States Treaty Series, 8–4

Weekly Law Reports, the, 2–3, 2–5
Where to Look for Your Law, 1–8
White Book, the. See Supreme Court Practice.
Words and Phrases Legally Defined, 6–15
World Treaty Index, 8–5

Year Books, 2–2
Yearbooks of International Law, 8–9

182